SYMBOLS AND ABBREVIATIONS USED

Good footpath (sufficiently distinct to be followed in ...)

Intermittent footpath (difficult to follow in mist)

No path; route recommended   ··············

Route on motor road   — unenclosed   — between walls   — between fences

Unenclosed road (off route)   ············

Wall ∞∞∞∞∞∞   Broken wall ∞ ∞ ∞ ∞   Fence ++++++++   Broken fence ''''''''''

Limestone clints   Crags   Scree   Boulders

Marshy ground   Trees

Cave or pothole •   Buildings   Contours (at 100' intervals) ·····1400···· ·····1300····

Summit-cairn ▲   Other (prominent) cairns △   Miles (from starting point) and direction of route ⑤

Stream or river (arrow indicates direction of flow)

Waterfall   Bridge   Railway   Map scale : 2" = 1 mile   North is top of the page

Abbreviations :   O.S. Ordnance Survey   Y.H.A Youth Hostels Association

WALKS IN LIMESTONE COUNTRY

THE PICTORIAL GUIDES
TO THE
LAKELAND FELLS

Publisher's Note

This book is a re-issue of the original volume written by A. Wainwright. The descriptions of the walks were correct, to the best of A. Wainwright's knowledge, at the time of first publication and are reproduced here without amendment at the wish of the Wainwright Estate. However, since certain footpaths, cairns and other waymarks described here may no longer be accurate, walkers are advised to check with an up-to-date map when planning a walk. Seeking local knowledge may be essential.

It should be noted further that fellwalking has increased dramatically since the time this guide was first published. Some of the more popular routes have become eroded and therefore good footwear and great care are necessary at all times. The vital points about fellwalking, as A. Wainwright himself wrote on many occasions, are: remember to watch where you are putting your feet, and use common sense.

WALKS
IN
LIMESTONE
COUNTRY

A Wainwright

footbridge,
Thorns Gill

PUBLISHED by FRANCES LINCOLN, LONDON

Frances Lincoln Limited
4 Torriano Mews
Torriano Avenue
London NW5 2RZ
www.franceslincoln.com

First published by Frances Lincoln
2003
Originally published by the Westmorland Gazette, 1970

Printed in Great Britain by Titus Wilson and Son, Kendal

ISBN O 7112 2237 1

To BETTY —

a charming companion

on these walks

INTRODUCTION

An observant traveller along the busy A.65 road from Skipton to Kendal will see little in the landscape to tempt him to halt his journey. Passing glances reveal that, north of the road for twenty miles or so, beyond a fringe of green pastures curiously fretted with white cliffs and rocky terraces, there extends a dark hinterland of desolate moors surmounted by an occasional peaked summit of no great height and remarkable only for its stark outline against the sky. If the traveller's destination is the Lake District, to which the road leads, nothing in view along the route appears to be worthier of attention, although he will look twice at Ingleborough and notice many beckoning signs that promise him natural wonders of cave and waterfall scenery if only he will turn aside.

Unlike the Lake District, where beauty is lavishly displayed all around and needs no seeking, the delights of this limestone countryside are not obviously in view. The delights are there, in full measure and in amazing variety, but they have to be sought on foot. It is a land of surprises. For the explorer there are places of fascinating interest, of strange beauty, of thrilling adventure, such as are not to be found elsewhere. This is a region unique, without a counterpart, but its charms are shyly hidden. Those who seek and find them are often enslaved. Yet few visitors come looking: the moors and the wild places remain quiet. The curlew cries and the lark sings, but there are few wanderers afoot to hear their call.

The appeal of a landscape may lie in its towering outlines or rich colours or verdant foliage or simple rural charm. But in general the limestone country lacks these attributes. What it has, and what is peculiar to it, is a wonderland created by its rocks: a chaotic assembly of glittering white crags and pinnacles and fissured pavements and crevices, sometimes beautiful, sometimes grotesque; as in no other place in the country, here the appeal is due primarily to its geology, to the earth movements of ages past, to the denudations of departed glaciers. Here geology lies naked and plain to see. Here a mass of carboniferous limestone some 600 feet thick is contorted dramatically by natural forces and pressures and extensive faulting, and into this permeable rock sink the mountain streams to dissolve the soft lime in the joints and so carve a fantastic underground honeycomb of passages, caves and potholes — a continual process that has no end. Elsewhere, landscapes are three dimensional; here is a fourth, deep into the earth. These abysmal subterranean gulfs are the province of the cave-explorer. Unlike our other native heights, about which there is little left to learn, man's knowledge of the limestone hills is in its infancy: an age of exploration awaits brave men, and their labours too will have no end. With speleology and geology, however, the ordinary walker is not actively concerned — his world is on the surface, in the light of day, and on the surface too are many features of absorbing interest: the scars, the clints, the ravines, the abandoned stream beds and the resurgences; and he may indulge the fascinating pastime of cave-hunting amongst the limestone outcrops and in the peaty hollows of the moors: this is an added interest, as is the alpine flora, in a region where the walking is delightfully easy, often on old grassgrown roads, often on velvet turf, and where the gradients are gentle. This is a part of England that should be better known by walkers who love quiet hills.

Which explains why the book has been written.

THE PLAN OF THE BOOK

Thirtyfour walks are described, each being the subject of a separate chapter. Every one has its particular charm or special objective. Together they form a network of routes — not necessarily paths — covering the most interesting parts of the area and providing the means of gaining a thorough appreciation of the scenery and a good knowledge of the geography.

Each of them returns the walker to his starting point. This arrangement has regard to the growing tendency of visitors to reach the district by car — with the gradual curtailments and withdrawals of public transport most walkers nowadays arrive on private wheels. The walks have therefore been planned with this in mind. Each walk starts at a place where cars can be parked and, whenever possible, avoids a retracing of steps over the same ground by giving an alternative route of return. Occasionally, but rarely, there is some overlapping of prescribed routes. Occasionally, and unavoidably, there is some walking to be done on hard roads, but never on busy roads: one delight of the area is the comparative peace and quiet of its minor byways, many of them still no more than country lanes between hedgerows. Walkers unburdened by cars who prefer to aim across country to fresh pastures can do so by linking routes together.

Most of the walks are fairly short in distance: half-day rather than full-day walks. This, too, recognises a current fashion — a happy one: that of family parties, youngsters and all, getting away from the car and exploring the hills and remote places of the countryside. Children will love these walks, but should not be allowed to stray. There are wonderful things to see — but there are hidden dangers, too, in the gleaming white cliffs and terraces of limestone.

Experience has shown that most walkers prefer to follow a diagram rather than a map, and, to cater for both tastes, route diagrams (which are not to scale) are given in addition to maps on a uniform scale of two inches to a mile. A key to the map symbols is provided inside the covers of the book, both front and back. For the use of readers who may wish to keep a personal account of their walks (or establish an alibi!) an outline 'log' is included towards the end of the book.

Care has been taken in planning the walks to ensure that private land is respected and avoided, if there are no rights of way, except where it has become common practice to pass over such land and no objection is raised; generally this applies to the rough ground above the intakes. If stopped and questioned by the occupier of the land, please don't argue on the authority of this book, which may well be wrong. Don't tell him "the book says so", for nothing will inflame his wrath more surely, besides landing the author in trouble. Retreat quietly, with apologies.... In his own field, a bull is always right. On his own land, a farmer is always right.

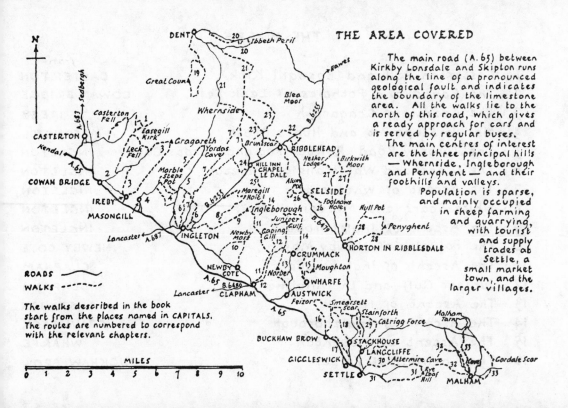

THE AREA COVERED

The main road (A.65) between Kirkby Lonsdale and Skipton runs along the line of a pronounced geological fault and indicates the boundary of the limestone area. All the walks lie to the north of this road, which gives a ready approach for cars and is served by regular buses.

The main centres of interest are the three principal hills — Whernside, Ingleborough and Penyghent — and their foothills and valleys.

Population is sparse, and mainly occupied in sheep farming and quarrying, with tourist and supply trades at Settle, a small market town, and the larger villages.

ROADS ⌇⌇⌇

WALKS - - - - - -

The walks described in the book start from the places named in CAPITALS. The routes are numbered to correspond with the relevant chapters.

MILES
0 1 2 3 4 5 6 7 8 9 10

THE WALKS

CASTERTON FELL AND EASEGILL KIRK

via BROWNTHWAITE PIKE, BULLPOT AND EASEGILL CAVES
returning via BULLPOT AND FELL ROAD

from CASTERTON

12¼ miles

Casterton Church

There are two good expeditions from Casterton: (a) the ascent of Casterton Fell and (b) a visit to Easegill Kirk (a limestone gorge, not a church). The approach to both is the same, and here they are linked in a single walk of great interest and contrasting variety.

From the top of the walled lane a grassy cart-track traverses the fellside, rejoining the motor road at a gate near Gale Garth; from this track a convenient detour may be made to the summits of Brownthwaite Pike and Casterton Fell (no path; on grass).

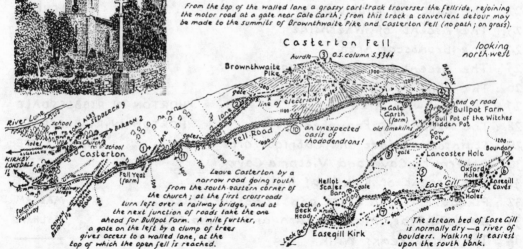

Casterton Fell

looking north-west

hurdle ③ O.S. column S.5344

Brownthwaite Pike

gate

line of electricity poles

BARBON

end of road

Bullpot Farm

Bull Pot of the Witches

Hidden Pot

Gale Garth (farm)

old limekiln

Cow Pot

an unexpected oasis of rhododendrons!

Lancaster Hole

Boundary Pot

Oxford Hole

Easegill Caves

Cow Holes

Ease Gill

River Lune

school

ROAD A683 SEDBERGH 9

BARBON 2

lane

Fell Road

hotel

church

school

KIRKBY LONSDALE

Casterton

Fell Yeat (farm)

Leave Casterton by a narrow road going south from the south-eastern corner of the church; at the first crossroads turn left over a railway bridge, and at the next junction of roads take the one ahead for Bullpot Farm. A mile further, a gate on the left by a clump of trees gives access to a walled lane, at the top of which the open fell is reached.

railway bridge

former railway

CONDAL BRIDGE

Hellot Scales Barn

gate

Leck Beck Head

Easegill Kirk

Leck Beck

The stream bed of Ease Gill is normally dry — a river of boulders. Walking is easiest upon the south bank.

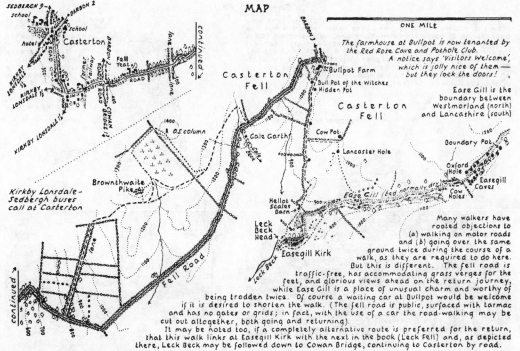

MAP

1
(2)

ONE MILE

The farmhouse at Bullpot is now tenanted by
the Red Rose Cave and Pothole Club.
A notice says 'Visitors Welcome',
which is jolly nice of them —
but they lock the doors!

Ease Gill is the
boundary between
Westmorland (north)
and Lancashire (south)

SEDBERGH 9
school
hotel
Casterton
Fell Yeat

DARBON 2

KIRKBY LONSDALE ROAD

COWAN BRIDGE ROAD

DARBON 2 ROAD

KIRKBY LONSDALE 1½

KIRKBY LONSDALE 1¾

lane

continued

Casterton
Fell

BARBON 3

Bullpot Farm
Bull Pot of the Witches
Hidden Pot

Casterton
Fell

Cow Pot
Lancaster Hole
Boundary Pot

Oxford
Hole
Easegill
Caves
Cow
Holes

O.S. column
Gale Garth
Gale Beck

Ease Gill (bed normally dry)

Brownthwaite
Pike

Kirkby Lonsdale-
Sedbergh buses
call at Casterton

Hellot
Scales
Barn

Leck
Beck
Head
Easegill Kirk

Leck Beck

Fell Road

continued

Many walkers have
rooted objections to
(a) walking on motor roads
and (b) going over the same
ground twice during the course of a
walk, as they are required to do here.
But this is different. The fell road is
traffic-free, has accommodating grass verges for the
feet, and glorious views ahead on the return journey,
while Ease Gill is a place of unusual charm and worthy of
being trodden twice. Of course a waiting car at Bullpot would be welcome
if it is desired to shorten the walk. (The fell road is public, surfaced with tarmac
and has no gates or grids; in fact, with the use of a car the road-walking may be
cut out altogether, both going and returning).

It may be noted too, if a completely alternative route is preferred for the return,
that this walk links at Easegill Kirk with the next in the book (Leck Fell) and, as depicted
there, Leck Beck may be followed down to Cowan Bridge, continuing to Casterton by road.

Casterton Fell

The big cairn on Brownthwaite Pike is conspicuously in view from the middle reaches of the Lune Valley, where it has the appearance of being the culminating point of Casterton Fell, a circumstance that leads to the assumption, wrongly, that it is the summit. The cairn is supported by a plinth, and stands in a wide surround of loose stones suggestive of a tumulus. The view is excellent, the highlights being the long skyline of the Lakeland peaks and the many graceful loops and curves of the Lune downriver from Kirkby Lonsdale.

A quarter-mile north-east of Brownthwaite Pike, the undulating top of Casterton Fell rises to a grassy hillock, which is surmounted by a triangulation column (S.5344), and this, at an altitude of 1436', marks the true summit of the fell.

The cairn on Brownthwaite Pike

Bullpot Farm

Lancaster Hole

The gaping chasm of Bull Pot of the Witches has been known since men settled in these parts, but the insignificant-looking Lancaster Hole is a recent (1946) discovery of much greater importance: it is, indeed, the key to an extremely extensive underground system of caves containing many rare and beautiful limestone formations, where continuing exploration has already accounted for six miles of passages and found alternative entrances from the stream bed in Ease Gill. The discovery of Lancaster Hole was a 'chance' find — a potholer resting nearby noticed a clump of grass quivering as if agitated by a breeze although the day was calm, and, curiosity leading to investigation, he encountered a strong draught issuing from a small hole in the ground: this was subsequently enlarged a little to permit entrance to a vertical shaft found to be 110 feet in depth, at the bottom of which access was gained to a vast series of wonderful caverns — a fantastic underworld of fairy grottoes with delicate calcite traceries, of immense halls with colonnades of massive stalagmites, of ceilings formed of myriads of slender opalescent stalactites, of floors and shelves littered with colourful cave pearls and crystals: the whole a treasure-house of supreme beauty that had been slowly developing through countless ages, and was now revealed to man; and those privileged adventurers who were the first to gaze upon these wonderful scenes were all profoundly impressed. The evidences below ground, in the size and nature of the formations and the superimposed layers of old stalagmitic deposits suggest that this is the oldest cave system in the country yet discovered.

Bull Pot of the Witches

The position of Bull Pot of the Witches is indicated by the trees surrounding it alongside the rough lane leading south from Bullpot Farm. The pothole engulfs the stream accompanying the lane and descends to a depth of 210 feet.

Lancaster Hole is situated amongst a few boulders in a green hollow of the moor 150 yards south of the wall containing Cow Pot. The entrance is closed by a manhole cover.

Lancaster Hole

Ease Gill

Ease Gill is ordinary — until it leaves the peaty moorland on which it has its beginnings and encounters limestone, whereupon its behaviour suddenly becomes quite extraordinary. Here its course is interrupted by huge rock steps in a steep-sided ravine made colourful by bracken, heather and trees: a lovely place, but eerily silent because the wide bouldery stream normally carries no water, the bed being bleached dry. The ravine has three sections: (a) upper Easegill, above a double waterfall deeply enclosed by sheer cliffs, where the stream, flowing gently down from Great Coum, reaches the limestone belt and sinks into rock crevices; (b) the middle reach, delightful but unexciting except for a tree-shaded dry waterfall; and (c) the spectacular Easegill Kirk, a deep gorge with vertical wooded cliffs and many caves and pools, at the end of which the underground stream reappears at the powerful resurgence of Leck Beck Head. In times of flood, however, the scene changes dramatically: the 'sinks' fill to the brim and cannot take more, the valley is pounded by a raging surface torrent, and, where there was silence, there is noise and tumult.

Upper Easegill

During the early exploration of Lancaster Hole it was realised that the subterranean passages were trending down the fellside in the direction of Ease Gill and confirmed when the Master Cave carrying the stream underground was located. Activity then shifted to the surface, to the bed of upper Easegill, where the stream was known to disappear at several points along its banks. All these 'sinks' were investigated in a lengthy siege and some were found, after much effort, to communicate directly with the Master Cave, forming a shorter way into it and opening up a through route to Lancaster Hole. Most are mere slits in the rocks, difficult to identify. A manhole cover at Oxford Hole marks the place of entry most commonly used. Although upper Easegill is full of interest and excitement for potholers, lesser fry such as timid walkers will find it unattractive, but they will not fail to admire the natural sculpture of Cow Holes, and the stream bed above the waterfall.

The waterfall at Cow Holes

The stream bed above the waterfall

Leck Beck Head

Most streams start from springs, little bubblings of water out of the ground. Leck Beck Head is a spring with a difference: it is a gusher, a strong uprising, a combined resurgence of many streams that have already flowed their respective ways across the surface of the open moorland only to sink in their beds upon meeting crevassed limestone, since when they have continued underground through the soft rock, following courses that potholers have been, in some cases, able to trace in part, but which prove generally to be impenetrable. At Leck Beck Head these subterranean waterways meet impervious rock and are forced out to daylight by pressure. The uprising here is the combined waters of the Easegill Caves, the Casterton Fell and many of the Leck Fell potholes. It is surprising that the point of emergence is not in the main bed of Ease Gill but in a side-valley.

In Easegill Kirk

Hellot
Scales
Barn

Don't look inside.
There may be dead bodies.

Leck Beck Head

THE CAVES AND POTHOLES OF LECK FELL

via BANK HOUSE AND LOST JOHN'S CAVE
returning via EASEGILL KIRK AND LECK BECK

from COWAN BRIDGE

7½ miles

CRAGARETH

looking south-east

Three Men
of Cragarath

The last
dwelling in
Lancashire,
and surely
the loneliest?

Leck Fell
House (farm)

Leck Fell

gate and sheep pens

ROAD

Lost John's
Cave

1300

1200

1100

1000

Peterson Pot
Smokey Hole

1100

shooting huts

1000

900

Easegill
Kirk

900

800

high stile

old limekiln ×

lane

to IREBY 1½

700

barn

gate

800

600

1 Short Drop Cave
2 Rumbling Hole
3 Rumbling Cave
4 Long Drop Cave
5 Eyeholes
6 Deaths Head Hole
7 Govel Pot
8 Ashtree Hole

Leck is a
pleasant and
peaceful refuge
from the busy A.65,
a place of noble trees
and quiet
parklands.

Leck Beck
Head

barn

LECK BECK

Anneside
(ruin)

gate

600

waterfalls

gate

600

Springs Wood

Bank House
(farm)

gate

ROAD

500

Leck
Mill

gate

Church
school

Ali

to IREBY 1

600

500

PARK HOUSE

gate

Leck Beck

Leck

700

former Clergy Daughters School,
Cowan Bridge, attended by the
four Brontë sisters, 1824-5.

This walk is wholly in Lancashire.

Take the road to
Leck and continue along it,
rising gradually, for 3 miles
to the open fell, where visit
the caves and potholes indicated and
descend to Easegill Kirk (a limestone gorge),
returning along the left bank of Leck Beck
on an improving path to Leck Mill.

Leck Mill was
a small corn mill.
The mill is no more;
the name lingers on.

COWAN
BRIDGE

INGLETON 4½
INGLETON 4½
BURROW

KIRKBY
LONSDALE 2½

Wild moorland and pleasant river scenery contribute equally
to this interesting expedition into lonely pothole territory.

MAP

2
(2)

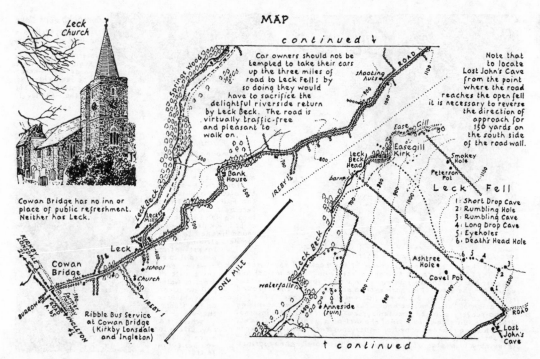

Leck
Church

Cowan Bridge has no inn or
place of public refreshment.
Neither has Leck.

continued ↓

Car owners should not be
tempted to take their cars
up the three miles of
road to Leck Fell; by
so doing they would
have to sacrifice the
delightful riverside return
by Leck Beck. The road is
virtually traffic-free
and pleasant to
walk on.

Note that
to locate
Lost John's Cave
from the point
where the road
reaches the open fell
it is necessary to reverse
the direction of
approach for
150 yards
on the
south side
of the road wall.

Leck Fell

1: Short Drop Cave
2: Rumbling Hole
3: Rumbling Cave
4: Long Drop Cave
5: Eyeholes
6: Death's Head Hole

ONE MILE

continued ↑

Ribble Bus Service
at Cowan Bridge
(Kirkby Lonsdale
and Ingleton)

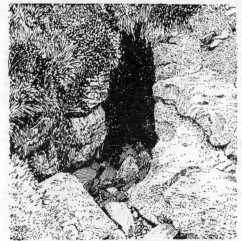

Rumbling Beck Cave

Rumbling Beck Cave engulfs a small stream and conveys it along a subterranean passage to Rumbling Hole, some 60 yards west, where it can be seen entering, as a waterfall, 30 feet below the moor level.

Rumbling Hole

Rumbling Hole is the largest surface opening on Leck Fell, pitting the moor to a depth of 365'.

Formerly it was given the alternative name of the Fairies Workshops, because of an incessant tapping noise rising out of its black depths — a sound likened to fairy hammers striking anvils. Investigation proved it to be, however, only the tinkle of drops of water falling upon musical stones on the floor of the hole.

Which is a pity. Life is so much fuller if you believe in fairies.

Lost John's Cave : the stream entrance

The best known and most extensive of the Leck Fell apertures is Lost John's Cave. There are two entrances (which unite inside), and it is possible by vigorous squirming for a non-expert who has little regard for the state of his garments to pass 20 yards underground from one to the other. But he should venture no further. The full exploration of Lost John's extended over several decades, resulting in the discovery of a complicated system of passages and internal potholes leading down to a final channel at a depth of 500 feet, where, having reached a bed of impervious rock, all the water in the Cave drains away in an uncharted and impenetrable canal — presumably to emerge at risings in Leck Beck and nearby springs.

Leck Beck

In normal weather, Leck Beck pursues a sedate course along a deeply-incurved and well-wooded valley, with an occasional waterfall to add spirit to its journey to the Lune, in surroundings that are quiet and unfrequented. Its source is a resurgence near Easegill Kirk, where the combined waters draining the vast basin of Great Coum rise after their underground passage through limestone. In flood conditions, however, the beck presents a quite different picture : then the limestone cavities soon fill to capacity, the spring is augmented by a torrent racing overland down Ease Gill, and the beck becomes a scene of angry and thunderous cataracts. Evidence of its force in spate is plentifully to be seen : in places the channel is carved to a width of fifty yards and choked by boulders, uprooted trees litter its bed and landslips are frequent —recent heavy floods have almost carried away part of the cart-track above Leck Mill, as illustrated below.

Waterfall, Leck Beck

THE ASCENT OF GRAGARETH

from IREBY

via LECK FELL
returning via IREBY FELL

7½ miles

Gragareth's challenging name and beckoning cairns
flatter to deceive, for its top is a long grassy
promenade with little of immediate interest.
It is a fine viewpoint, however, and the
ascent should therefore be reserved
for a day of clear visibility.

*Leave Ireby by the Leck road, but at
Todgill take the rough lane ahead,
which leads pleasantly to
the tarred road going to
Leck Fell House, where a
steep scramble followed
by a trudge over a
desert of grass
brings the top
underfoot.*

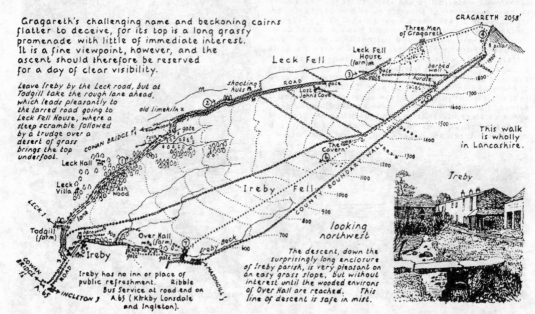

This walk
is wholly
in Lancashire.

*looking
northwest*

The descent, down the
surprisingly long enclosure
of Ireby parish, is very pleasant on
an easy grass slope, but without
interest until the wooded environs
of Over Hall are reached. This
line of descent is safe in mist.

Ireby has no inn or place of
public refreshment. Ribble
Bus Service at road-end on
A.65 (Kirkby Lonsdale
and Ingleton).

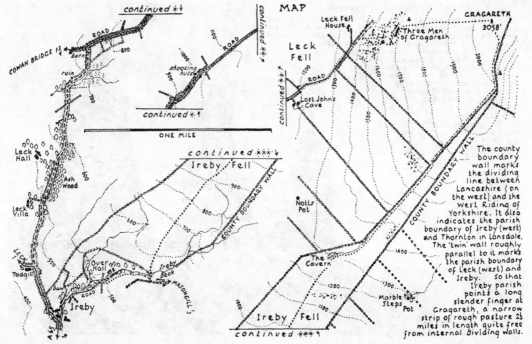

MAP

3
(2)

continued ✳✝

ROAD

COWAN BRIDGE 1¾

barn

800

ruin

700

600

ONE MILE

ROAD

continued ✳✳✳

shooting
huts

500

continued ✳✝

Leck
Hall

Ash
Wood

500

Leck
Villa

continued ✳✳✳ ↓
Ireby Fell

COUNTY BOUNDARY WALL

900

800

700

600

500

Leck R.

500

Todgill

400

Overend
Hall

barn

500

ROAD

Ireby
Beck

MASONGILL 3

A65

Ireby

1000

1100

1200

1300

Ireby Fell

continued ✳✳✳

Leck Fell House

Leck
Fell

ROAD

1600

1500

1700

Three Men
of Cragareth

GRAGARETH
2058'

1900

2000

1800

1600

1700

1500

continued ✳✳✳

Lost John's
Cave

1400

1500

Notts
Pot

The
Cavern

1400

1200

1300

Marble
Steps Pot

1100

COUNTY BOUNDARY WALL

The county
boundary
wall marks
the dividing
line between
Lancashire (on
the west) and the
West Riding of
Yorkshire. It also
indicates the parish
boundary of Ireby (west)
and Thornton in Lonsdale.
The 'twin' wall roughly
parallel to it marks
the parish boundary
of Leck (west) and
Ireby.   so that
Ireby parish
points a long
slender finger at
Gragareth, a narrow
strip of rough pasture 2½
miles in length quite free
from internal dividing walls.

The Three Men of Gragareth

How much more satisfying, and how much more inspiring, are the rugged cairns built by lovers of mountains than the smooth concrete columns erected by the makers of maps! The first have individual character; the latter, conforming to a pattern, have none.

The Three Men of Gragareth have been a notable landmark for many generations, even earning recognition by name on Ordnance maps. They stand on the edge of a rash of stones at the top of the steep rise overlooking Leck Fell House, the occupier of which must feel a proprietary interest in the gaunt figures that share his lonely world.

The summit of Gragareth

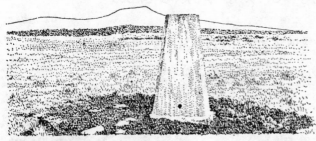

The summit of Gragareth, crowned by the Ordnance Survey with a concrete column (Nº S. 5404), is everywhere grassy, tediously so, with an eroded peat-stack and the boundary wall as the only other nearby items of interest. The distant view, however, is excellent: the Lune Valley, Morecambe Bay and the Lakeland hills, westwards, are all well displayed, while higher fells close the panorama in other directions at nearer range, Ingleborough and Whernside in particular being prominent. The summit rises half a mile due east of the Three Men, whose company is to be preferred if a halt for sandwiches is intended.

The Cavern

The Cavern (also known as Ireby Fell Cavern) was long thought to be only an insignificant opening in the floor of a large shakehole, but explorations in post-war years have revealed a vast system of passages and shafts going down 400 feet below the surface.

Over Hall

MARBLE STEPS POT AND HUNT'S CROSS

from MASONGILL

6¼ miles

A pleasant traverse along the crest of a typical limestone escarpment.

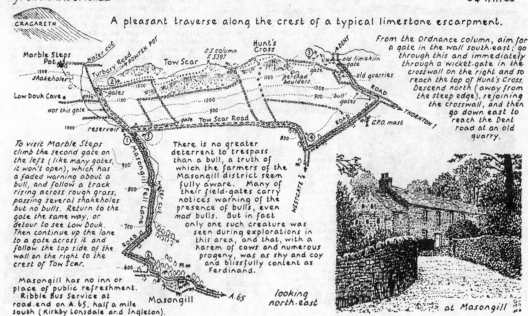

CRAGARETH

Marble Steps Pot
water cut
Turbary Road
ROWTEN POT
shakeholes
1200
Tow Scar
O.S.column
5397
Hunt's
Cross
DENT
old limekiln
gate
old quarries
Low Douk Cave
2
gates
1100
1200
1000
perched boulders
1100
1000
900
'bull' gates
ROAD
3
gate
DENT
From the Ordnance column, aim for a gate in the wall south-east; go through this and immediately through a wicket-gate in the crosswall on the right and so reach the top of Hunt's Cross. Descend north (away from the steep edge), rejoining the crosswall, and then go down east to reach the Dent road at an old quarry.

NOT THIS GATE
1000
reservoir
gate
Tow Scar Road
900
1
800
4
ROAD
THORNTON!
G.P.O. mast

To visit Marble Steps climb the second gate on the left (like many gates, it won't open), which has a faded warning about a bull, and follow a track rising across rough grass, passing several shakeholes but no bulls. Return to the gate the same way, or detour to see Low Douk. Then continue up the lane to a gate across it and follow the top side of the wall on the right to the crest of Tow Scar.

Masongill has no inn or place of public refreshment. Ribble Bus Service at road-end on A.65, half a mile south (Kirkby Lonsdale and Ingleton).

Masongill Fell Lane
900
800
water cut
700
ROAD
600

WESTGATE?

There is no greater deterrent to trespass than a bull, a truth of which the farmers of the Masongill district seem fully aware. Many of their field-gates carry notices warning of the presence of bulls, even mad bulls. But in fact only one such creature was seen during explorations in this area, and that, with a harem of cows and numerous progeny, was as shy and coy and blissfully content as Ferdinand.

Masongill
A.65

looking north-east

at Masongill

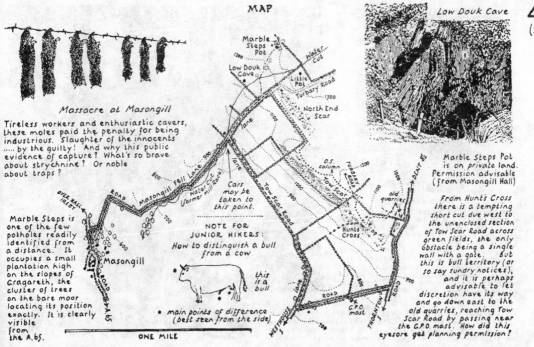

MAP

4
(2)

Low Douk Cave

Massacre at Masongill

Tireless workers and enthusiastic cavers, these moles paid the penalty for being industrious. Slaughter of the innocents ..... by the guilty! And why this public evidence of capture? What's so brave about strychnine? Or noble about traps?

Marble Steps is one of the few potholes readily identified from a distance. It occupies a small plantation high on the slopes of Gragareth, the cluster of trees on the bare moor locating its position exactly. It is clearly visible from the A.65.

NOTE FOR JUNIOR HIKERS:
How to distinguish a bull from a cow

this is a bull

• main points of difference (best seen from the side)

ONE MILE

Marble Steps Pot is on private land. Permission advisable (from Masongill Hall)

From Hunt's Cross there is a tempting short cut due west to the unenclosed section of Tow Scar Road across green fields, the only obstacle being a single wall with a gate. But this is bull territory (or so say sundry notices), and it is perhaps advisable to let discretion have its way and go down east to the old quarries, reaching Tow Scar Road by passing near the G.P.O. mast. How did this eyesore get planning permission!

Marble Steps Pot

Water Cut

Low Douk Cave

Little Pot

Turbary Road

North End Scar

Lane

Cars may be taken to this point.

Water Cut (former Mill Race)

Masongill Fell Lane

ROAD

GYLE HALL (FELL)

Masongill

ROAD A.65

O.S. column

Turbary Road

Tow Scar

Tow Scar Road

old quarries

DENT 85

Hunts Cross.

WESTHOUSE Lane

ROAD

G.P.O. mast

THORNTON ROAD

The Water Cut

An untidy little watercourse, crossed in
the rough pasture below Marble Steps Pot,
is unlikely to attract attention although at
this point channelled into field drains. It
is an artificial water cut, formerly a mill
race, and a triumph of primitive civil
engineering. Originally it captured the
Cragareth streams destined to die in the
Kingsdale potholes, diverting their waters
along the contours to provide a supply for
cottages and mills in the Greta valley.

Marble Steps Pot

One of the better-known potholes, Marble Steps has a
long history of exploration, the greatest depth reached
being 400 feet below the surface. It takes its name from
the black limestone staircase, polished by water action.

THE TURBARY ROAD, ROWTEN POT AND YORDAS CAVE
via THORNTON HALL and HUNT'S CROSS
returning via KELD HEAD and THORNTON FORCE

from INGLETON

9½ miles

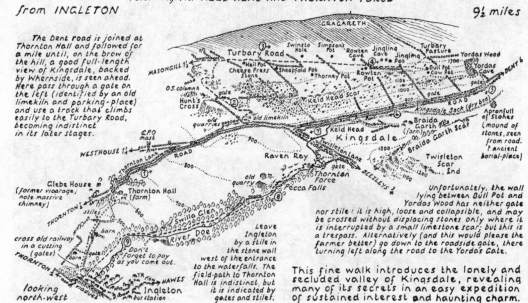

The Dent road is joined at Thornton Hall and followed for a mile until, on the brow of the hill, a good full-length view of Kingsdale, backed by Whernside, is seen ahead. Here pass through a gate on the left (identified by an old limekiln and parking-place) and use a track that climbs easily to the Turbary Road, becoming indistinct in its later stages.

Glebe House
(former vicarage; note massive chimney)

cross old railway in a cutting (gates)

looking north-west

Leave Ingleton by a stile in the stone wall west of the entrance to the waterfalls. The field-path to Thornton Hall is indistinct, but it is indicated by gates and stiles.

Don't forget to pay as you come out.

Unfortunately, the wall lying between Bull Pot and Yordas Wood has neither gate nor stile: it is high, loose and collapsible, and may be crossed without displacing stones only where it is interrupted by a small limestone scar; but this is a trespass. Alternatively (and this would please the farmer better) go down to the roadside gate, there turning left along the road to the Yordas Gate.

Apronfull of Stones (mound of stones, seen from road. ? ancient burial-place)

This fine walk introduces the lonely and secluded valley of Kingsdale, revealing many of its secrets in an easy expedition of sustained interest and haunting charm.

MAP

5
(2)

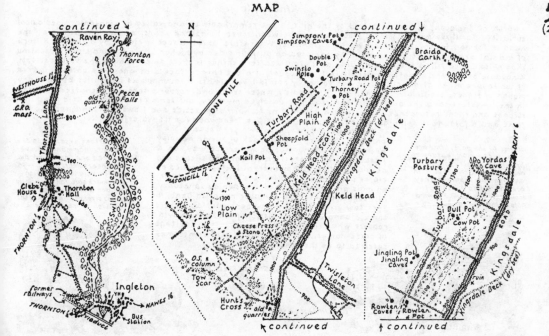

continued ↓

continued ↓

N

Raven Ray

Thornton Force

WESTHOUSE 1½

G.P.O. mast

Pecca Falls

old quarries

Thornton Lane

800

Twisleton Glen

River

THORNTON LANE

700

Glebe House

Thornton Hall

600

500

former railways

THORNTON

Viaduct

Ingleton

Y.H.

Bus Station

HAWES 16

Simpson's Pot
Simpson's Caves

Braida Garth

Double J Pot

Swinsto Hole

Turbary Road Pot

Thorney Pot

Turbary Road

High Plain

Keld Head Scar

1200

1100

1000

Kingsdale Beck (dry bed)

Kingsdale

MASONGILL 1½

Sheepfold Pot

Kail Pot

ONE MILE

1300

Low Plain

Cheese Press Stone

1200

Keld Head

Turbary Pasture

1100

1000

Yordas Cave

DENT 6

O.S. column

Tow Scar

1000

900

Twisleton Lane

Turbary Road

Bull Pot

Cow Pot

ROAD

Kingsdale

Jingling Pot
Jingling Cave

Hunt's Cross

old quarries

ruin

Rowten Caves

Rowten Pot

Kingsdale Beck (dry bed)

↑ continued

↑ continued

Kingsdale

North of Ingleton, hidden in a fold of the hills, is the remarkable upland valley of Kingsdale, a geological curiosity. For three miles its level floor extends between steep limestone scars, as straight as a die; the head is formed by the sprawling western flanks of Whernside and the foot is closed by a smooth hillock of glacial drift, so that this is a valley enclosed on all four sides by higher ground: conditions indicating that a lake once filled the hollow. Only at its south-eastern corner is there an escape for the valley stream, Kingsdale Beck. And Kingsdale Beck itself is unusual: it is the only surface drainage for a gathering area of ten square miles of moorland subject to heavy rainfall yet almost throughout its length its bed is a dry ribbon of stones, artificially channelled. Kingsdale's water seeps underground through uncharted fissures in the limestone and the outlet of much of it is an unsolved mystery, but some re-appears at Keld Head in a strange and silent resurgence, after which it conforms to normal practice and flows overland, soon to win fame and a fortune in shillings as the beautiful River Doe, renowned for its waterfalls.

Kingsdale is quiet, with two farmsteads the only habitations, and the lack of human activity and absence of murmuring waters convey, on a first visit, an impression of brooding silence and desolation that is, however, quickly dispelled on closer acquaintance: life here is as it should be; animals graze undisturbed, birds enjoy sanctuary. Although traversed by a motor road (to Dent) it sees few visitors. But many centuries ago there came a band of special visitors from Scandinavia, robbers who became settlers and left a heritage of place-names.... Kingsdale is still sometimes referred to as the Valley of the Vikings.

Relics of the past, kilns are a very common feature of limestone country, occurring not only in quarries but often on open outcroppings. They are all built to pattern, the stone being deposited down a hole in the roof for burning.

Limestone exposed to the weather commonly becomes fissured and contorted, but the Cheese Press Stone — 15 tons in weight and 9' high — is remarkable for its smooth surface and angular shape. It was stranded in its present location by ice movement.

Limekiln and stone hut, old quarry, Hunts Cross.

Cheese Press Stone,
Low Plain
(Grid Ref: 688762)

The attractions of the Turbary Road

The Turbary Road, a grassy cart-track, was used originally to convey peat from the Turbary Pasture (above Yordas Cave) in the exercise of common rights, but a present-day visitor might be excused for thinking it was designed as a promenade for the inspection of caves and potholes, which occur on both sides in abundance. The 'road' follows the easiest line along a natural shelf (and forms, incidentally, an excellent terrace for walkers): it so happens that, on the same contour, streams coming down from Gragareth reach the permeable limestone and promptly sink in the clefts and crevices they have carved. Some of these holes lead to labyrinths of underground passages and caverns descending nearly 400 feet to the level of the floor of Kingsdale, where the combined waters emerge to daylight at the Keld Head uprising. Swinsto Hole and Simpson's Pot in particular are extensive subterranean systems, although their surface apertures are quite insignificant and not worth seeking. Rowten Pot, however, is different. Rowten Pot compels a halt.

the surface opening

Rowten Cave

the stream entrance

The Rowten System

The first thing likely to be noticed at Rowten is a surprising hole in the ground on the edge of the track, with a stream sliding along its floor 15 feet below; this hole is the collapsed roof of Rowten Cave, the entrance to which is 100 yards west across the moor, where an opening in the clints reveals a surface stream dropping down rocky steps and disappearing underground. (Note a dry passage, the former course of the stream, directly opposite the cave entrance: this continues for 80 feet to its exit on the moor, with an intermediate exit at 70 feet, and is good fun. Children may safely be let loose in this, and will enjoy it). The main cave can be followed downstream by intrepid grown-ups with torches at the cost of wet feet and personal discomfort: it is not dangerous and, except for two short crawls, not difficult. Daylight is next seen at the hole by the track, then, in darkness, Jingling Cave joins in on the left and a turn to the right leads again to daylight in Rowten Pot (pictured overleaf). <u>Go no further.</u> Scramble up steep rocks on the left to safety on the moor.

underground line of cave = ...

stream Jingling Pot

Jingling Caves

collapsed roof of cave

wall

stream

Rowten Caves

mini cave

Turbary Road

wall

gate and folds

Rowten Pot

collapsed roof of cave

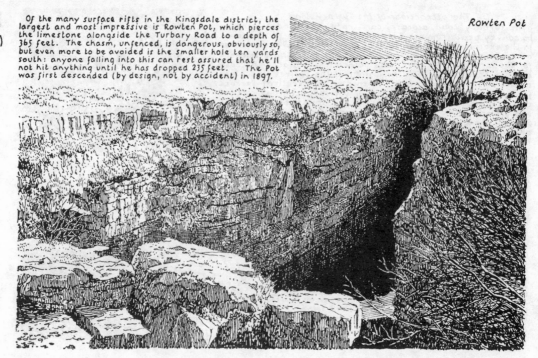

5
(5)

Of the many surface rifts in the Kingsdale district, the largest and most impressive is Rowten Pot, which pierces the limestone alongside the Turbary Road to a depth of 365 feet. The chasm, unfenced, is dangerous, obviously so, but even more to be avoided is the smaller hole ten yards south: anyone falling into this can rest assured that he'll not hit anything until he has dropped 235 feet. The Pot was first descended (by design, not by accident) in 1897.

Rowten Pot

Yordas Cave

Yordas Cave was formerly a showplace, visited only by permission from Braida Garth farm and on payment of an admission charge. It has long been known, one name inscribed therein bearing the date 1653. Now it is open for inspection by any who pass that way: few do. The cave cannot be seen from the road below and is not indicated by notices: it is hidden from sight in a plantation 150 yards above a roadside gate. Entrance to the cave is made down stone steps to a low man-made arch on the left of a rocky ravine amongst the trees. A torch is necessary for its exploration; the better the torch the more will be seen of the many natural sculpturings. The floor is of mud: mostly firm mud, but muddy mud near the subterranean stream. Wait inside the entrance for a few minutes until the eyes become attuned to the blackness of the interior, then go forward 25 bold strides (or, more likely, 50 faltering steps; take care not to collide with 'dangling' rocks) to reach the stream running on a pebbly bed: hereabouts the roof is loftiest, some 60 feet above; this is the Great Hall of Yordas.

PLAN

Turn right, upstream, to the cave's principal attraction: the Chapter House, a circular chamber into which cascades an elegant waterfall, this strange and beautiful scene being viewed through a remarkable open 'window' in a wall of rock. Most of the other natural features are in this vicinity: the Eagle, the Pulpit, the Great Organ, the Giant's Arm, the Map of Wales, some requiring not only a bright illuminant but a fanciful imagination for their recognition. The stream flows through the Great Hall to vanish in a small opening not big enough to take all the water when in spate — hence the cave floods after heavy rain.

Yordas, according to legend, was the name of a Nordic giant with a liking for hunting small boys and devouring them in this cave. What a strange thing to do !! Why not small girls ?

The entrance

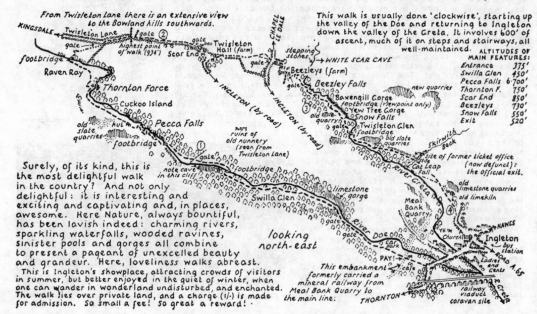

From Twisleton Lane there is an extensive view to the Bowland hills southwards.

KINGSDALE · Twisleton Lane · gate ② · gate · Twisleton Hall (farm) · highest point of walk (934') · Scar End · CHAPEL LE DALE · stepping stones · → WHITE SCAR CAVE · gate · footbridge · gate · Raven Ray · Thornton Force · Cuckoo Island · Pecca Falls · footbridge · old slate quarries · hut · INGLETON (by road) · INGLETON (by road) · Beezleys (farm) · Beezley Falls · new quarries · Baxengill Gorge footbridge (viewpoint only) · Yew Tree Gorge · Snow Falls · Twisleton Glen · footbridge · old slate quarries · gate · old quarry · ruins of old nunnery (seen from Twisleton Lane) · ① · gate · note cave in this cliff · footbridge · Swilla Glen · Skirwith Beck · Cat Leap Fall · RIVER GRETA · site of former ticket office (now defunct): the official exit. · old limestone quarries · old limekiln · limestone gorge · Meal Bank Quarry · ④ · ③ · gate · gate · River Doe · looking north-east · car park · PAY! · cafe · YH · Church · Ladies and Gents · Ingleton · bus station · A65 · HAWES · CRETA · This embankment formerly carried a mineral railway from Meal Bank Quarry to the main line: THORNTON · railway viaduct · caravan site

This walk is usually done 'clockwise', starting up the valley of the Doe and returning to Ingleton down the valley of the Greta. It involves 600' of ascent, much of it on steps and stairways, all well-maintained.

ALTITUDES OF MAIN FEATURES:

Entrance	375'
Swilla Glen	450'
Pecca Falls 6	700'
Thornton F.	750'
Scar End	850'
Beezleys	730'
Snow Falls	550'
Exit	520'

Surely, of its kind, this is the most delightful walk in the country? And not only delightful: it is interesting and exciting and captivating and, in places, awesome. Here Nature, always bountiful, has been lavish indeed: charming rivers, sparkling waterfalls, wooded ravines, sinister pools and gorges all combine to present a pageant of unexcelled beauty and grandeur. Here, loveliness walks abreast.

This is Ingleton's showplace, attracting crowds of visitors in summer, but better enjoyed in the quiet of winter, when one can wander in wonderland undisturbed, and enchanted. The walk lies over private land, and a charge (1/-) is made for admission. So small a fee! So great a reward!

Twisleton Hall and Scar End

MAP

N

Lone

Raven Ray

Thornton Force

Twisleton Scar 1100

1000

Scar End

Twisleton Hall 800

CHAPEL 2½

Pecca Falls

old quarry

800

nunnery (ruin)

700

Beezleys

RIVER Greta

stepping stones

Beezley Falls

Baxengill Gorge

Yew Tree Gorge

Snow Falls

Oddies Lane (motor road)

old quarries

River Doe

600

600

Skirwith Beck

Meal Bank

Cat Leap Fall

500

old quarry

old quarry

former railways

YH

Ingleton

Viaduct

Bus Station

HAWES 16

400

ONE MILE

The waterfalls, beautifully and bewitchingly set in wooded glades and rocky gorges, are the principal attraction of the Ingleton glens, but plain to see too are the evidences of the geological evolution that created them. In both glens, the rivers, coming down from the hills, have carved deep channels through the surface limestone, exposing hard underlying rocks of slate and gritstone impervious to water, over which they rush in cataracts and cascades to the lower level of the Ingleton plains: these channels, sheltered from wind and storm, have encouraged a wealth of trees and ferns. Just north of Ingleton, and greatly influencing the landscape, is the line of the Craven Fault, a major dislocation: it is crossed on this walk at the entrance to Swilla Glen and at Meal Bank Quarry, and at both places the tilt of the limestone strata, sinking underground to the south, is in full view; in both places, too, the thickness of the limestone cap is clearly revealed in vertical cliffs exceeding 200 feet in height. But, in both glens, this limestone barrier is succeeded further upstream by colourful slate formations, as old quarries testify and as is noticeably evident on or near the paths, particularly in the vicinity of Pecca Falls. At the head of the glens, on the open moor, limestone is again dominant, extending on all sides in characteristic clints and outcroppings.

Of the two glens, the more frequented westerly one, containing the Doe, is the more charming and lovely; the easterly one is, however, much the grander and more romantic, the greater volume of water of the Greta restlessly pounding the black walls of the gorges beneath a canopy of trees. Locally the river in the eastern glen is known as the Twiss (derived from Twisleton), but the Ordnance Survey recognise it only as the Greta, a name it retains after being joined by the Doe on its further journey to the Lune.

6
(3)

Pecca Twin Falls   *Pecca Falls*   Holly Bush Spout

Thornton Force

— the highest of the Ingleton waterfalls, has a sheer drop of 46 feet. Its setting is charming, the rocky cliffs forming a natural amphitheatre below a fringe of trees. Here the River Doe falls over a limestone crag lying on a foundation of older slate rocks.

Beezley Falls form a series of cascades in a rocky bed as the River Greta, after a tranquil and leisurely journey from the limestone of God's Bridge, rushes in wild confusion down a ravine constricted greatly by boulders and cliffs and rugged outcrops.

Nearby, but happily out of sight, is a huge quarry recently opened for the extraction of 'green granite' (a handsome stone, but more blue than green and more slate than granite), and the former peace of the glen, where once the only sounds were of birds and leaping waters, is now disturbed by the industrial noise of stone-crushing machinery, an unwelcome distraction.

Beezley Falls

Baxengill Gorge

Snow Falls

The other waterfalls depicted in this chapter occur on the two main rivers in the glens, but Cat Leap Fall is the final ecstatic plunge of a small tributary of the Greta, Skirwith Beck. It is not seen from the path but can be visited by a brief detour.

6
(6)

Cat Leap Fall

THE ASCENT OF WHERNSIDE
via THE SOUTH-WEST RIDGE
returning via ELLERBECK

14¼ miles

The full length of Whernside's south-west ridge, from the confluence of the rivers Greta and Doe to the summit, is traversed on this ascent and, with a variation, repeated on the descent. There is little excitement about it but it is an exhilarating walk, a tonic for jaded minds and a splendid exercise for the legs. It is also a challenge to those who doubt their ability to walk fourteen miles.

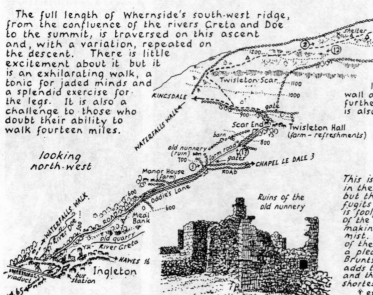

looking north·west

The Standing Stone is a huge limestone boulder built into the wall and overtopping it. 350 yards further along, another big boulder is also built into the wall; over it, at this point, a natural ring of limestone boulders is so symmetrically arranged as to suggest a manmade stone circle.

This is the longest walk described in the book.* The walking is easy but the miles are long and tempus fugits quickly. The southwest ridge is foolproof in any weather because of the accompanying unbroken wall, making the ascent perfectly safe in mist. To avoid a complete reversal of the route for the return journey a pleasant variation is given, via Bruntscar and Ellerbeck, but this adds to distance and time and effort, and the ridge is the easiest and the shortest way back to Ingleton.

* excepting the Three Peaks Walk

Ruins of the old nunnery

Map labels: continued • Standing Stone • boulder in wall • 1300 • fluted pothole • shelter • Ewes Top • 1300 • Scales Moor • 1200 • ② • ⑫ • Twisleton Scar • 1100 • KINGSDALE • 1000 • gate • WATERFALLS WALK • Scar End • barn • Twisleton Hall (farm – refreshments) • 800 • old nunnery (ruin) • 700 • farm road • ⑪ • gates • CHAPEL LE DALE 3 • Manor House (farm) • ① • ROAD • 600 • Oddie's Lane • ROAD • Meal Bank • 600 • WATERFALLS WALK • old quarry • River Doe • YH • River Greta • NAWES 16 • Ingleton • bus station • A.65 • viaduct

The summit of Whernside, 2419', is the highest elevation reached in this series of walks. An Ordnance column (Nº 2982, without the usual prefix S) occupies the site of a former cairn. The panorama is comprehensive, including much of the Dales country and the hills of Lakeland. York Minster has been proved to be in view by an exchange of flashing signals.

From the wall near Sand Beds Head Pike the summit of Whernside comes fully into view, with Low Pike and High Pike seen as prominent rises.

Note that the limestone wall ends around 1300' above Rigg Side, this being the upper limit of the limestone strata, and is succeeded by a gritstone wall continuing to the summit.

Sand Beds Head Pike

High Pike

Low Pike

...ure projecting through stones in wall as a stile.

looking north-west

shelter

West Fell

Combe Scar

Rigg Side

continued ↑

Ellerbeck (farm)

Hodge Hole (store)

Broadrake (farm)

old sheepfold

Scales Moor

fenced boghole

ford

gate

gates

old kiln

barn

Bruntscar (farm)

CHAPEL LE DALE

HILL INN CHAPEL LE DALE

Only a brief written description of the route is needed to supplement the diagram, the ascent being straightforward and uncomplicated.

Leave Ingleton by the 'middle road' between the two rivers, passing the gas holder, and, after a mile, take the farm road to Scar End. (If a car is available, three road-miles and an hour's time can be saved by parking it, with permission, at Scar End). Turn left at Scar End up a stony lane (familiar to those who have 'done' the waterfalls walk, and who hasn't?). 150 yards beyond the gate take a smooth grass path bifurcating on the right. This is a 'made' path, delightful to follow to Ewes Top after which it deteriorates. The Standing Stone is prominent and the path should be left at a fluted pothole to go across to it. The wall is then a perfect guide to the summit.

Descending, return to the foot of Low Pike and there turn left down rough pastures to Bruntscar, whence continue past Hodge Hole to Ellerbeck. At the ford a path strikes across Scales Moor parallel to the descending ridge, and although it is narrow and in places indefinite there is no difficulty on this easy terrain in rejoining the route of ascent at the fluted pothole.

There is a fine cave behind the old farmhouse at Bruntscar. Unfortunately there is no time to go and see it.

7
(3)

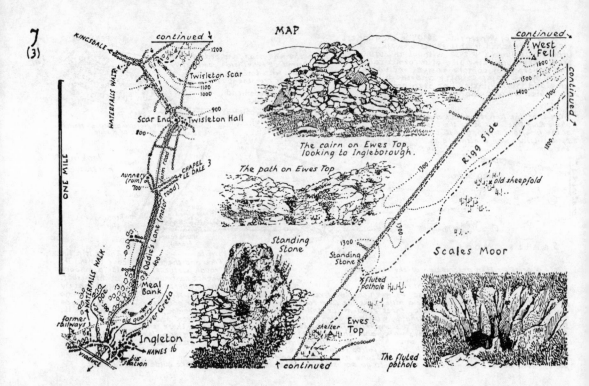

MAP

ONE MILE

KINGSDALE

WATERFALLS WALK

continued ↓

1200

Twisleton Scar

1100

1000

900

Scar End · Twisleton Hall

800

nunnery (ruin) 700

CHAPEL LE DALE 3

farm road

Oddie's Lane (motor road)

600

Meal Bank

WATERFALLS WALK

500

old quarry

former railways

River Greta

viaduct

Ingleton

HAWES 16

bus station

The cairn on Ewes Top, looking to Ingleborough.

The path on Ewes Top

Standing Stone

1300

Standing Stone

1300

Ewes Top

shelter

continued ↓

continued →

West Fell △ 1600

continued ↓

1500

1400

1300

Rigg Side

old sheepfold

Scales Moor

fluted pothole

The fluted pothole

1200

MAP

7
(4)

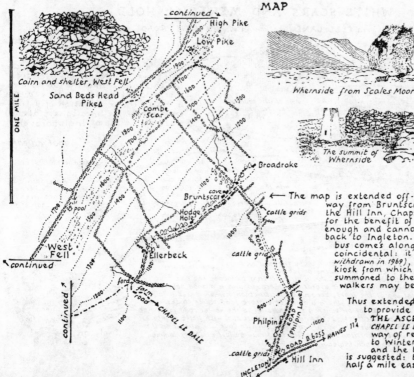

ONE MILE

continued
High Pike
Low Pike

Cairn and shelter, West Fell

Sand Beds Head Pike △

Combe Scar

WHERNSIDE 2419'

Whernside from Scales Moor

The summit of Whernside

High Pike
continued

Broadroke

Bruntscar

cattle grids

Hodge Hole

West Fell
continued

Ellerbeck

cattle grids

ford
farm road
CHAPEL LE DALE
continued

Philpin

ROAD (Philpin Lane)

ROAD B6255   HAWES 11½

cattle grids

Hill Inn

INGLETON 4¼

← The map is extended off-route to indicate the way from Bruntscar to the main road at the Hill Inn, Chapel-le-Dale, especially for the benefit of those who have had enough and cannot face the long walk back to Ingleton. At the Hill Inn, if a bus comes along it will be more than coincidental: it will be uncanny (*service withdrawn in 1969*), but there is a telephone kiosk from which an Ingleton taxi can be summoned to the rescue. Impoverished walkers may be able to thumb a lift.

Thus extended, the map also serves to provide the complete route of THE ASCENT OF WHERNSIDE *from CHAPEL LE DALE*, and for a variation way of return the direct descent to Winterscales (*see Walk Nº 23*) and the tarmac road therefrom is suggested: this road joins the B6255 half a mile east of the Hill Inn.

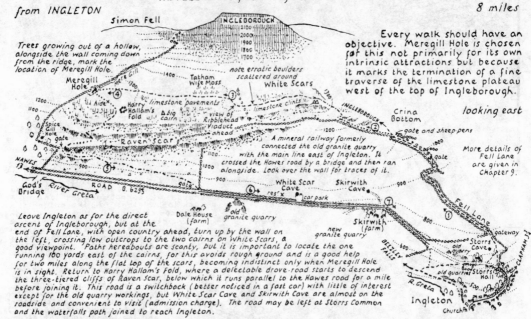

looking east

More details of
Fell Lane
are given in
Chapter 9.

Every walk should have an objective. Meregill Hole is chosen for this not primarily for its own intrinsic attractions but because it marks the termination of a fine traverse of the limestone plateau west of the top of Ingleborough.

Trees growing out of a hollow, alongside the wall coming down from the ridge, mark the location of Meregill Hole.

note erratic boulders scattered around White Scars

A mineral railway formerly connected the old granite quarry with the main line east of Ingleton. It crossed the Hawes road by a bridge and then ran alongside. Look over the wall for traces of it.

Leave Ingleton as for the direct ascent of Ingleborough, but at the end of Fell Lane, with open country ahead, turn up by the wall on the left, crossing low outcrops to the two cairns on White Scars, a good viewpoint. Paths hereabouts are scanty, but it is important to locate the one running 100 yards east of the cairns, for this avoids rough ground and is a good help for two miles along the flat top of the scars, becoming indistinct only when Meregill Hole is in sight. Return to Harry Hallam's Fold, where a delectable drove-road starts to descend the three-tiered cliffs of Raven Scar, below which it runs parallel to the Hawes road for a mile before joining it. This road is a switchback (better noticed in a fast car) with little of interest except for the old quarry workings, but White Scar Cave and Skirwith Cave are almost on the roadside and convenient to visit (admission charge). The road may be left on Storrs Common and the waterfalls path joined to reach Ingleton.

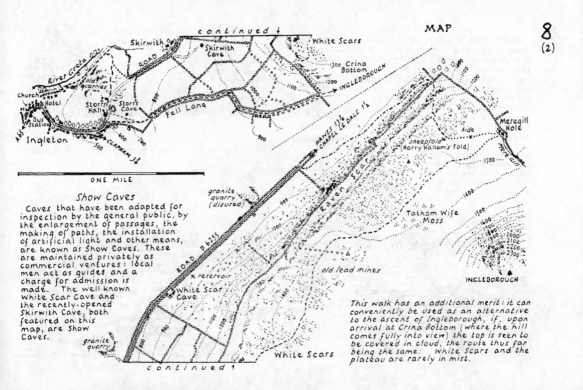

MAP

8
(2)

continued ↓

Skirwith

White Scars

Skirwith Cave

1300 Crina Bottom

INGLEBOROUGH → 1200

River Greta

ROAD

1100

Church
Hotel

old quarries

Storrs Hall

Storrs Cave

Fell Lane

1200

Bus Station

Ingleton

A65

CLAPHAM 3½

600

500

900

HAWES 1¾   CHAPEL LE DALE 1½

Raven Scar

Meregill Hole

hide

sheepfold
(Harry Hallam's Fold)

Fire Gill

1700

Tatham Wife Moss

1400

1600
1700
1800
1900
2000
2100
2200
2300

INGLEBOROUGH

ONE MILE

Show Caves

Caves that have been adapted for inspection by the general public, by the enlargement of passages, the making of paths, the installation of artificial light and other means, are known as Show Caves. These are maintained privately as commercial ventures: local men act as guides and a charge for admission is made.   The well-known White Scar Cave and the recently-opened Skirwith Cave, both featured on this map, are Show Caves.

granite quarry (disused)

900

ROAD B6255

× reservoir

White Scar Cave

900

1100

granite quarry

800
900

old lead mines

This walk has an additional merit: it can conveniently be used as an alternative to the ascent of Ingleborough, if, upon arrival at Crina Bottom (where the hill comes fully into view) the top is seen to be covered in cloud, the route thus far being the same.   White Scars and the plateau are rarely in mist.

White Scars

continued ↓

White Scars

White Scars is an elevated plateau between the Hawes road and Ingleborough's summit-dome, a midway halt on the western slope of the mountain: it is the roof of a well-known cave 600 feet below. Large areas of it are covered by surface limestone, which is not usually associated with metallic minerals, but at one time there were leadmines here, obviously not greatly exploited, the traces being scanty. The valley side of the plateau is bounded by the triple escarpment of Raven Scar, the longest unbroken cliff in the district.

The cairns of amateurs — on White Scars

Ingleborough, from White Scars

The cairn of a professional

— above Raven Scar

Meregill Hole

Meregill Hole is one of the major chasms, its passages descending to a depth of 520 feet below the moor, but its appearance is less awesome than many others, being concealed by trees. There are three apertures within a wire fence. A peculiarity of Meregill Hole is that the trend of the underground cavities is not towards the valley but back into the heart of Ingleborough, below the stream that feeds it.

THE ASCENT OF INGLEBOROUGH

DIRECT, via CRINA BOTTOM
returning via the same route

from INGLETON : 7½ miles there and back

Ingleborough, the 'beacon hill', is the undisputed overlord of the limestone country, the most compelling presence. It has the advantage, which few mountains have, of a bold and challenging outline from whatever direction it is seen, and, because it rises in isolation from valleys on all sides, the facility of looking higher than it is. When Ingleborough is in view, it is a magnet for the eyes. And for the feet of the adventurous.

There can be few days in the year when the summit has no visitors, for Ingleborough is probably the most-ascended mountain in the country outside Lakeland, and the ascent described here is second only to the tourist walk around the glens and waterfalls of Ingleton as the most-trodden route in this book.

INGLEBOROUGH 2373'

slope of wet peaty grass

Quaking Pot

Green Springs

White Scars

Crina Bottom

Greenwood Pot

former rifle range

gate and pens

Hard Gill

Rantry Hole

Lane fit for cricket

Fell Lane is usually the muddiest part of the ascent.

Fell Lane

Lane cluttered with stones from broken wall

gate

HAWES 15¼

Storrs Cave

gateway

An embedded rock in the lane at this point is indicated on large-scale Ordnance maps as 'Giant's Grave'

Storrs Hall

60 yards short of the gateway the path crosses a grass embankment (now indistinct) that formerly carried a mineral railway from the disused granite quarry on the Hawes road

line of former railway

Ingleton

Church

CLAPHAM 3¾

Bus Station

Police : this is where you'll get locked up if you don't behave yourselves

looking north-east

Hard Gill is normally dry, the water from Green Springs sinking near Greenwood Pot

White Scars gives its name to the famous cave, here about 600 feet beneath the surface.

Greenwood Pot was named after the late Mr Tom Greenwood, first manager and an early explorer of White Scar Cave; at this point an excavation was undertaken in an unsuccessful attempt to discover a passage down into the Cave from the surface, following the stream.

Good Yorkshiremen do this climb as a duty of their inheritance — and find it a pleasure, as will all 'foreigners' too. It is a fine walk on a fine day and full of reward.

MAP

9
(2)

Not only has Ingleborough a commanding appearance. It is a mountain of many talents and surely the most interesting of all British heights. The summit, which has been both a native settlement and a military post, is a place for the archaeologist. The views are magnificent. The crags are the habitat of rare Alpine plants. It is the happiest of hunting grounds for the geologist and especially the speleologist. And for the humble walker it provides, with its satellites, twenty square miles of gloriously fascinating wandering in a unique terrain. The summit is the objective of an annual fell race and a key point in the Three Peaks Walk.

Routes of return

For the purposes of this chapter, the return walk is assumed to retrace in its entirety the outward route, there not being a convenient alternative way back to Ingleton.

But if time and energy permit, the descent may be made to Clapham *via* Gaping Gill, a beautiful journey. (*Hourly bus from Clapham to Ingleton*). See Chapter 11 for the route.

continued

The Ordnance surveyors refer to Ingleborough as *Ingleborough Hill* on their maps. Nobody else does. *Ingleborough* is enough. Indeed, even *Ingleborough* is superfluous for Ingleton folk, who affectionately call it *The Hill*, as though recognising no other.

ONE MILE

Storrs Cave

continued

Most people do this walk unaware of the proximity to the path of certain caves and potholes, but, with the exception of Quaking Pot, these are not spectacular.

What is usually known as *Storrs Cave* is an old mine working, the original cave having been covered over. *Rantry Hole*, marked by a tree, is now blocked by debris. *Greenwood Pot* is a narrow aperture in the stream bank: the path actually 'strides' across it. *Quaking Pot* is the middle one of three holes close together at 1430'.

9
(3)

Crina Bottom and Ingleborough

The limestone cliffs of Ingleborough

A collar of limestone surrounds the gritstone summit of Ingleborough at the 2150'-2200' contour. This is noticeable, but not pronounced, where the path climbs through it, but a simple walk to the north along a grass terrace above the shattered escarpment leads in 200 yards to a section that has best resisted erosion and survives as a steep crag.

It is here, in crannies of the rocks, that the purple saxifrage may be found in flower in late April, although the display is scanty compared with that on Penyghent's white cliffs. To take these shy plants is to kill them — they are creatures of the hills; in town gardens they pine and die. So don't.

Quaking Pot

Quaking Pot pierces the moor near the path, at 1430', but will not be seen unless sought. There are three holes in close proximity. Quaking Pot is the circular middle one, with a fernclad shaft into which trickles a small waterfall. Nearby is an attractive double shakehole spanned by a natural bridge. Just beyond is a large untidy sinkhole, in the bottom of which a vertical shaft is concealed by a covering of iron sheets: this is the point of entry into the Quaking Pot underground system now in favour. All potholing activity here has the object of establishing a surface link with the wellknown White Scar Cave, far below ground at this point.

The geology of Ingleborough

It is the geology, the bare bones, of Ingleborough that contributes most to its special attractions, and the essential features of its structure are evidenced by the surface rocks during the ascent from Ingleton.

The base of the mountain is composed of ancient pre-Cambrian rocks and it is on these that Ingleton stands, owing a considerable prosperity to the liberal supplies of coal, slate and so-called granite extracted.

After leaving the road at Storrs Hall, carboniferous limestone (also known as mountain or scar limestone) is seen in the outcrops, in the boulders, in the stone walls and in the white scars above Crina Bottom. This belt of limestone, some 600 feet thick and lying on the older rocks, visibly surrounds the final slopes on all sides. It is permeable, the lime content being soluble, so that the streams flowing down from the higher ground are, upon reaching it, all engulfed, sinking under the surface to continue their journey to the impervious base (there to emerge from caves or springs) by forming the waterworn passages that are the peculiar delight of the potholer. Unlike other popular mountains, whose every nook and cranny has long been charted, Ingleborough releases its secrets slowly, and a thousand years of exploration will not disclose all its underground mysteries.

This plinth of carboniferous limestone supports a cone of conglomerate rocks, predominantly shale and sandstone, generally concealed by a covering of peat but revealed in the crags and screes of the escarpments, the second of which is manifestly a layer of limestone sandwiched between coarser rocks.

This upper strata persists almost to the top of the mountain but is finally crowned by a shallow cap of millstone grit, forming the summit.

MILLSTONE GRIT (100' thick)

escarpments   summit

SHALES

SANDSTONE

Ingleton

CARBONIFEROUS LIMESTONE

SLATES · COAL

The summit of Ingleborough

The summit is a broad plateau, slightly tilted, half a mile in circumference, and carpeted with dry turf: a place not endowed by nature with especially exciting features yet having many objects of interest provided by man. Inevitably there is a column erected by the Ordnance Survey, just like all the others except for its number (S.5619); there is a well-built cross-wall wind shelter, equipped in its centre with a very helpful, detailed view indicator erected in 1953 by the Ingleton Fell Rescue Team, but which, being above eye level, may not be noticed; and between them a large cairn. Where the path from Ingleton reaches the summit-rim 50 yards away an even larger cairn welcomes the climber; this has a singular history, being the site of a battlemented round tower (a hospice) built in 1830, at which the jollifications on the day of its opening ceremony became so alcoholic that parts of it were thrown down there and then, the rest being destroyed later: the curved stones of the base can still be seen. A walk across the top, observing the ground with care, will reveal the circular foundations of the huts that suggest to archaeologists a native settlement of the first men in the district, and along the northern and eastern edges, very clearly seen, is the shattered wall of the military camp, believed to be Roman. Two large cairns on the perimeter indicate the points where paths to Clapham and Chapel-le-Dale leave the summit.

The view is far-reaching, and superb — but there are very few days of visibility so good that all the details on the view indicator can be checked, unfortunately!

site of hospice

shelter

gateway in wall

hut circles

o.s. column

A : to Ingleton
B : to Chapel-le-Dale
C : to Clapham

0   100 YARDS   200   300

Summit Features

top left : site of hospice
top right : wind shelter and
view indicator
left : Ordnance column and cairn
right : ruins of military wall
below : foundations of circular hut

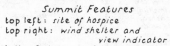

THE POTHOLES OF NEWBY MOSS

from NEWBY COTE

4 miles

The easy climb up to Newby Moss is tedious, in uninspiring surroundings, but two of the potholes, Fluted Hole and Pillar Holes, are botanical gems on the barren moor and worth a visit.

Newby Cote

Go up the lane alongside the hamlet on the west, past an old quarry and through a gate to the open moor. The good track soon fades, but go round the corner of the wall on the left (looking over it to see an old limekiln) and follow it until a stone shooting hide is reached, then turn right to find the small sinkhole into which Grey Wife Sike formerly disappeared. The sike is now dry in this section, taking the form of a shallow cut or channel. Follow this uphill, passing a ruined shooting box. If the line of the sike is in doubt, take direction from the nearby shooting hides. The slope soon eases, giving easy walking to the upper sinkhole, which now engulfs the water of Grey Wife Sike. At this level precisely turn left to Fluted Hole and continue in the same direction to Pillar Holes and Long Kin West Pot, the latter being preceded by Fern Pot and other depressions. A rutted cart-track is found at Long Kin West Pot, actually crossing it, and this leads pleasantly down to the old road near Cold Cotes, providing excellent views of Ingleton and beyond. The old road is quiet, and there is little danger of being run over, but if there is objection to walking on tarmac, note that the hillside can be crossed on the descent to give an alternative return above the intake wall, so rejoining the outward route near the limekiln.

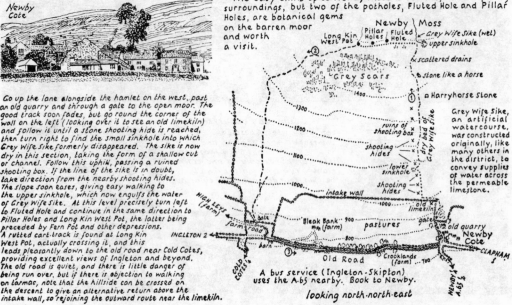

Newby Moss

Long Kin West Pot
Pillar Holes
Fluted Hole
Grey Wife Sike (wet)
upper sinkhole

× scattered drains

× stone like a horse

Grey Scars

Harryhorse Stone

1400

1300

1200

1100

1000

ruins of shooting box

dry bed of Grey Wife Sike

shooting hides

lower sinkhole

shooting hides

intake wall

HIGH LEYS (farm)

farm road

gate

Bleak Bank (farm)

900

pastures

800

gate

old limekiln

barn

INGLETON 2

COLD COTES 1

Old Road

700

Crooklands (farm)

old limekiln

old quarry

Newby Cote

CLAPHAM 3

NEWBY 1
A.65 1½

A bus service (Ingleton-Skipton) uses the A.65 nearby. Book to Newby.

looking north-north-east

Grey Wife Sike, an artificial watercourse, was constructed originally, like many others in the district, to convey supplies of water across the permeable limestone.

MAP

10
(2)

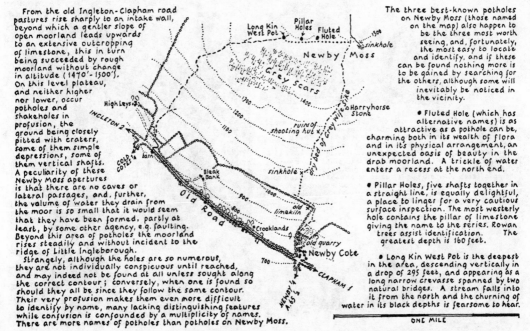

From the old Ingleton-Clapham road pastures rise sharply to an intake wall, beyond which a gentler slope of open moorland leads upwards to an extensive outcropping of limestone, this in turn being succeeded by rough moorland without change in altitude (1470'-1500'). On this level plateau, and neither higher nor lower, occur potholes and shakeholes in profusion, the ground being closely pitted with craters, some of them simple depressions, some of them vertical shafts. A peculiarity of these Newby Moss apertures is that there are no caves or lateral passages, and, further, the volume of water they drain from the moor is so small that it would seem that they have been formed, partly at least, by some other agency, e.g. faulting. Beyond this area of potholes the moorland rises steadily and without incident to the ridge of Little Ingleborough.

Strangely, although the holes are so numerous, they are not individually conspicuous until reached, and may indeed not be found at all unless sought along the correct contour; conversely, when one is found so should they all be since they follow the same contour. Their very profusion makes them even more difficult to identify by name, many lacking distinguishing features while confusion is confounded by a multiplicity of names. There are more names of potholes than potholes on Newby Moss.

The three best-known potholes on Newby Moss (those named on the map) also happen to be the three most worth seeing, and, fortunately, the most easy to locate and identify, and if these can be found nothing more is to be gained by searching for the others, although some will inevitably be noticed in the vicinity.

● Fluted Hole (which has alternative names) is as attractive as a pothole can be, charming both in its wealth of flora and in its physical arrangement, an unexpected oasis of beauty in the drab moorland. A trickle of water enters a recess at the north end.

● Pillar Holes, five shafts together in a straight line, is equally delightful, a place to linger for a very cautious surface inspection. The most westerly hole contains the pillar of limestone giving the name to the series. Rowan trees assist identification. The greatest depth is 160 feet.

● Long Kin West Pot is the deepest in the area, descending vertically in a drop of 295 feet, and appearing as a long narrow crevasse spanned by two natural bridges. A stream falls into it from the north and the churning of water in its black depths is fearsome to hear.

ONE MILE

Is this Harryhorse Stone?

Harryhorse Stone, so named on Ordnance large-scale maps, is approached in expectancy that the name derives from its resemblance to a horse, but when reached it is found to be merely a large fissured block of limestone, isolated in the moorland grass. No horse ever looked like this.

But, 250 yards further, there comes into sight a grey mare, sitting motionless on her haunches in the grass, which upon being offered a titbit turns out to be another isolated rock, curiously carved by the weather. This is not indicated on maps.

Is it possible that the Ordnance Survey have appended the name to the wrong stone?

Or this?

Fluted Hole

Pillar Holes

Long Kin West Pot

THE ASCENT OF INGLEBOROUGH

from CLAPHAM   *via GAPING GILL ; returning via the same route*   *9 miles there and back*

From the bridge carrying the A65 over Clapham Beck take the road along the west side of the beck to the top of the village, where a notice indicates a cottage at which tickets can be obtained (6d) for the mile-long walk through the private grounds of the Ingleborough Estate, this forming the first part of the journey. (Non-affluent walkers can avoid the admission charge by using instead the adjacent lane to Clapdale Farm, thence rejoining the route by a footpath beyond the end of the private section). The grounds, which include an attractive lake, are delightfully furnished with trees and shrubs and served by an excellent path (Ingleborough Drive), which becomes public at a gate and continues past a simple waterworks to the imposing entrance of Ingleborough Cave and the resurgence of Beck Head. The valley continues ahead, still wooded and no less well-defined but now without a surface stream, and turns left into the striking ravine of Trow Gill, the towering walls of which come close together at its head, suggesting that the boulders littering the floor may once have formed the roof of a cave. The path climbs out of the gill, over the boulders, and goes on for a further half-mile, still in a dry valley and now accompanying a wall, to a prominent stile giving access to the open moorland. A track, becoming indistinct, curves right to the fenced crater of Gaping Gill, and here Fell Beck is followed (upstream!) for 100 yards before the route turns away to make a beeline for the stony end of the ridge of Little Ingleborough with the main summit now in view and easily reached at its south-east corner by a distinct path.

INGLEBOROUGH 2373'

Little
Ingleborough

*looking
north-west*

2200
2100
2000
1900
1800
1700
1600
1500
Fell Beck
1400

Disappointment Pot

Gaping Gill

Flood Entrance Pot

Bar Pot

stile

1300

1200
1100
1000
900

If a different route is required for the return journey the obvious one is the direct descent to Ingleton (Chapter 9) (hourly bus to Clapham) — but no way back is better than the way here described ; there may even be eagerness to re-visit the many wonderful places already seen on the ascent. Besides, that ticket you bought will take you back through the grounds without further charge.

Clapdale
(farm)

Ingleborough
Cave

Foxholes

Trow Gill

gate and stile

Grotto

lane to
Clapdale
Farm

cottage
for tickets

Clapdale Wood

gate

800

Beck Head

Clapham Beck

800

Clapham

A65

Church

The Lake

700

Ingleborough Hall

Hotel (New Inn)

Garage

SETTLE 6½

Of the many walks described in this book, the ascent of Ingleborough from Clapham is pre-eminent, the finest of all, a classic. A lovely village..... charming woodlands....... an enchanting valley .... natural wonders .... a climb to a grand mountain-top. Oh yes, this is the best.

MAP

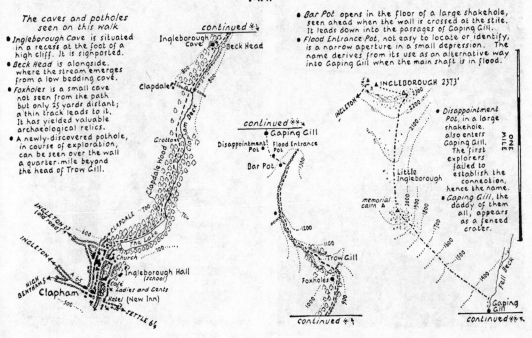

The caves and potholes seen on this walk

- *Ingleborough Cave* is situated in a recess at the foot of a high cliff. It is signposted.
- *Beck Head* is alongside, where the stream emerges from a low bedding cave.
- *Foxholes* is a small cave not seen from the path but only 25 yards distant; a thin track leads to it. It has yielded valuable archaeological relics.
- A newly-discovered pothole, in course of exploration, can be seen over the wall a quarter-mile beyond the head of Trow Gill.

- *Bar Pot* opens in the floor of a large shakehole, seen ahead when the wall is crossed at the stile. It leads down into the passages of Gaping Gill.
- *Flood Entrance Pot*, not easy to locate or identify, is a narrow aperture in a small depression. The name derives from its use as an alternative way into Gaping Gill when the main shaft is in flood.

- *Disappointment Pot*, in a large shakehole, also enters Gaping Gill. The first explorers failed to establish the connection, hence the name.
- *Gaping Gill*, the daddy of them all, appears as a fenced crater.

continued **

Ingleborough Cave   Beck Head

Clapdale

Grotto

Clapdale Wood   Clapham Beck

800

700

continued ***   Gaping Gill

Disappointment Pot   Flood Entrance Pot

Bar Pot

INGLETON 3½ (old road)

CLAPDALE   700

INGLETON 4

600

The Lake

700

Church

Ingleborough Hall (school)

HIGH BENTHAM 5

A 65

Café
Ladies and Gents
Hotel (New Inn)

Clapham

500

SETTLE 6½

▲ INGLEBOROUGH 2373'

INGLETON

2300

2300

2200

2100

Little Ingleborough

2000

memorial cairn ▲

1800

1700

1200

1100   Trow Gill

1000   Foxholes   900

1000   900

Fell Beck

1600

1500

1400

Gaping Gill

ONE MILE

continued ***   continued ***

Clapham

Ingleborough Drive

The entrance to the Grotto

The Grotto is one of several ornamental features in the grounds of Ingleborough Hall but it is the natural beauties of tree and shrub and water that endow Clapham and its environs with such distinctive charm. The Farrer family occupied the Hall for several generations and cherished at all times a deep regard for the scenic attractiveness of their estate and also a concern in the welfare of the village, to which they contributed many benefactions. Reginald Farrer (1880-1920) established a high international reputation as a botanist, particularly as an authority on alpine plants.

Ingleborough Cave

Ingleborough Cave, also known as Clapham Cave, is the oldest of the show caves, having been made accessible to the public since the discovery of its inner passages in 1837. An admission charge is made and a guide and a lantern provided.

The stream emerging nearby at Beck Head, and thereafter known as Clapham Beck, is the one that falls into Gaping Gill, a mile away, under the name of Fell Beck, having in the meantime pursued an underground course, partly through Ingleborough Cave. This has been proved by colouration tests, but the evidence is circumstantial only as the actual course of the stream below the surface has not yet been followed by man (not for want of trying). Progress has been made at both ends, a passage in Gaping Gill having been traced beyond Bar Pot, while Ingleborough Cave has long been known to extend almost to Trow Gill. The half-mile between these limits of exploration remains a mystery, but someday, no doubt, the link will be made and a subterranean passage established from Beck Head to Gaping Gill.

Beck Head Bridge

Trow Gill

Gaping Gill

Trow Gill and the dry valley

There seems little doubt that the ravine of Trow Gill was fashioned by running water long ago, and that the dry valley leading into and out of it at one time contained the stream that now finds an underground way from Gaping Gill to Beck Head. The caves and potholes are geologically so much more ancient than the surface contours, however, that one must assume for an explanation that they were, at the end of the ice age and for long thereafter, blocked by glacial mud, forcing the stream to carve a new passage overland (the present dry valley) until erosion of the glacial debris again exposed the cavities and admitted the stream to its former channels.

Gaping Gill

Gaping Gill is the best-known of all British potholes and its fame is international. The surface rift is spectacular and awesome: the bottom of a grassy crater forms a vertical shaft that drops 340 feet, straight as a plumbline, engulfing a stream (Fell Beck) and widening into a gigantic chamber, of cathedral proportions, from the floor of which an extensive labyrinth of passages branches off, over three miles of these underground channels already having been surveyed. The stories of the discovery and exploration of its underworld make fascinating reading. The first attempt to descend the shaft was made in 1842 but not until 1895 was the floor of the pothole reached (by rope ladder), exploration having since proceeded continuously. The usual method of descent nowadays is by steel cable, chair and winch after diverting the stream into side-channels. Unlike many major potholes, which are screened by trees or descend in stages, the surface appearance of Gaping Gill is starkly simple and severe and its dangers are palpably and appallingly obvious. Keep children and dogs under lock and key. On no account should a visitor try to look straight down the shaft, as the author is doing in the picture, the silly old so and so. He ought to have more sense, at his age.

This handsome cairn on the ridge of Little Ingleborough is hidden from sight by the curve of the western slope but found by a brief detour. It has a built-in tablet, inscribed A.A.S. 1928. The old track here comes from Cold Cotes via Newby Moss.

The long climb up to the ridge from Gaping Gill eases off at the ruins of a sheepfold, with the summit of Ingleborough now seen ahead.

Details of the summit of Ingleborough are given in Chapter 9.

JUNIPER GULF AND THE ALLOTMENT

via LONG LANE ; returning via CLAPDALE

from CLAPHAM

8 miles

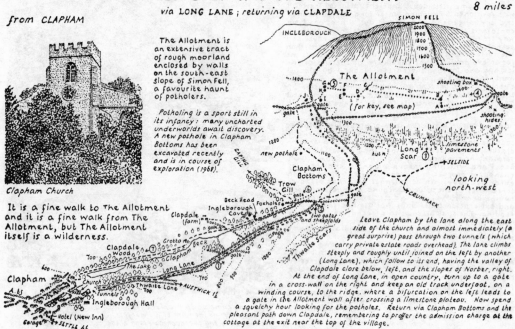

Clapham Church

The Allotment is an extensive tract of rough moorland enclosed by walls on the south-east slope of Simon Fell, a favourite haunt of potholers.

Potholing is a sport still in its infancy: many uncharted underworlds await discovery. A new pothole in Clapham Bottoms has been excavated recently and is in course of exploration (1968).

It is a fine walk to The Allotment and it is a fine walk from The Allotment, but The Allotment itself is a wilderness.

Leave Clapham by the lane along the east side of the church and almost immediately (a great surprise) pass through two tunnels (which carry private estate roads overhead). The lane climbs steeply and roughly until joined on the left by another (Long Lane), which follow to its end, having the valley of Clapdale close below, left, and the slopes of Norber, right. At the end of Long Lane, in open country, turn up to a gate in a cross-wall on the right and keep an old track underfoot, on a winding course, to the ridge, where a bifurcation on the left leads to a gate in the Allotment wall after crossing a limestone plateau. Now spend a squelchy hour looking for the potholes. Return via Clapham Bottoms and the pleasant path down Clapdale, remembering to proffer the admission charge at the cottage at the exit near the top of the village.

MAP

12
(2)

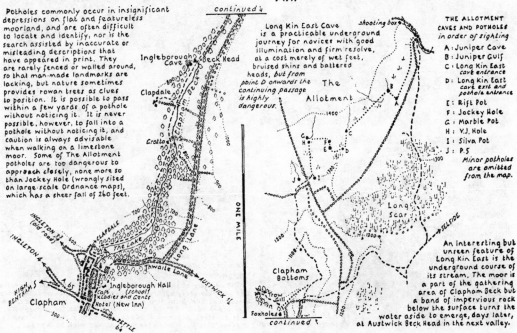

Potholes commonly occur in insignificant depressions on flat and featureless moorland, and are often difficult to locate and identify, nor is the search assisted by inaccurate or misleading descriptions that have appeared in print. They are rarely fenced or walled around, so that man-made landmarks are lacking, but nature sometimes provides rowan trees as clues to position. It is possible to pass within a few yards of a pothole without noticing it. It is never possible, however, to fall into a pothole without noticing it, and caution is always advisable when walking on a limestone moor. Some of The Allotment potholes are too dangerous to approach closely, none more so than Jockey Hole (wrongly sited on large-scale Ordnance maps), which has a sheer fall of 260 feet.

continued ↓

Long Kin East Cave is a practicable underground journey for novices with good illumination and firm resolve, at a cost merely of wet feet, bruised shins and battered heads, *but from point D onwards the continuing passage is highly dangerous.*

THE ALLOTMENT CAVES AND POTHOLES in order of sighting

A : Juniper Cave
B : Juniper Gulf
C : Long Kin East cave entrance
D : Long Kin East cave exit and pothole entrance
E : Rift Pot
F : Jockey Hole
G : Marble Pot
H : Y.J. Hole
I : Silva Pot
J : P.5

Minor potholes are omitted from the map.

Ingleborough Cave
Beck Head
Clapdale
Clapham Beck Head
Grotto
The Allotment
1400
shooting box
Long Scar
SELSIDE
1300
1200
1300
Clapham Bottoms
1200
Trow Gill
Foxholes

ONE MILE

INGLETON 3½ (old road)
INGLETON 4
CLAPDALE
The Lake
Long Lane
Thwaite Lane
AUSTWICK 1½
HIGH BENTHAM 5
A 65
Ingleborough Hall
Cave (school)
Ladies and Gents
Hotel (New Inn)
SETTLE 6¼
Clapham
500
600
700
700
800
800
900
1000

An interesting but unseen feature of Long Kin East is the underground course of its stream. The moor is a part of the gathering area of Clapham Beck but a band of impervious rock below the surface turns the water aside to emerge, days later, at Austwick Beck Head in the next valley.

continued ↓

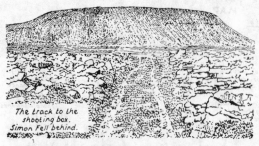

The track to the
shooting box.
Simon Fell behind.

Juniper Cave

Juniper Gulf

The dangers of the fearful abyss of Juniper Gulf are concealed
and not outwardly apparent; indeed, the surface opening, into
which a stream falls, is a little maze of crevices of some charm,
a pleasant oasis in the dreary moor.   But below, unsuspected,
vast cavities descend 420 feet, where the stream vanishes in
impenetrable fissures to reappear at Austwick Beck Head.

Long Kin East: Cave exit and pothole entrance

Rift Pot

The entrance to Long Kin East Cave occurs where a streamlet crosses the peaty moor to reach surface limestone and slides down a long watersmoothed channel to vanish underground. The cave forms a continuous winding passage for a quarter of a mile (twice the surface distance) before debouching into the lower depths of Rift Pot. But, 160 yards overland SSW, in a green patch amongst outcrops, it briefly admits daylight, at the hole illustrated above (probably formed by a collapse of the roof). Here the cave is 15 feet down, and this point is generally regarded as its exit, the continuation forward to Rift Pot being given the name of Long Kin East Pot.

The long narrow cleft of Rift Pot has not been formed by the action of water, as is usual, but is a fault-fissure, the entrance being quite dry although underground streams do discharge into the cavity at lower levels. This pothole is the second deepest in The Allotment, the floor of the final chamber being 320 feet below the surface of the moor.

WALK
13

THE ASCENT OF NORBER
via THE NORBER BOULDERS; returning via CRUMMACK

from AUSTWICK

5 miles

An easy climb to a pleasant summit
—but it is the famous Boulders
that will be most remembered.

looking north-west

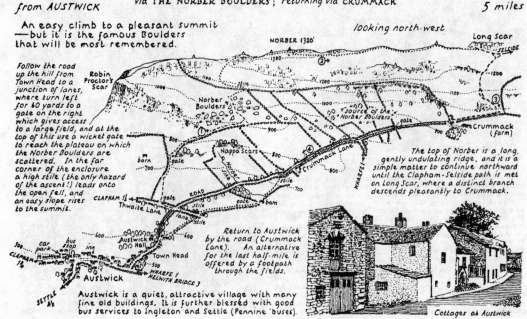

Follow the road
up the hill from
Town Head to a
junction of lanes,
where turn left
for 60 yards to a
gate on the right
which gives access
to a large field, and at the
top of this use a wicket gate
to reach the plateau on which
the Norber Boulders are
scattered. In the far
corner of the enclosure
a high stile (the only hazard
of the ascent!) leads onto
the open fell, and
an easy slope rises
to the summit.

The top of Norber is a long,
gently undulating ridge, and it is a
simple matter to continue northward
until the Clapham-Selside path is met
on Long Scar, where a distinct branch
descends pleasantly to Crummack.

Return to Austwick
by the road (Crummack
Lane). An alternative
for the last half-mile is
offered by a footpath
through the fields.

Austwick is a quiet, attractive village with many
fine old buildings. It is further blessed with good
bus services to Ingleton and Settle (Pennine 'buses).

Cottages at Austwick

MAP

13
(2)

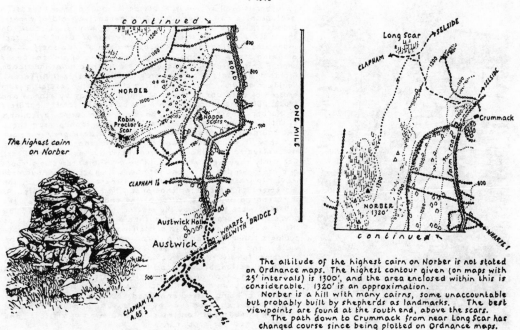

The highest cairn on Norber

continued →

Long Scar → SELSIDE
CLAPHAM
SELSIDE
Crummack
farm road
NORBER
1320'
continued →
WHARFE !

NORBER
ROAD
Robin Proctor's Scar
Nappa Scars
CLAPHAM 1½
ONE MILE
Austwick Hall
WHARFE 1
HELWITH BRIDGE 3
Austwick
CLAPHAM 1½
A.65 3
SETTLE 4½
A.65 4½

The altitude of the highest cairn on Norber is not stated on Ordnance maps. The highest contour given (on maps with 25' intervals) is 1300', and the area enclosed within this is considerable. 1320' is an approximation.

Norber is a hill with many cairns, some unaccountable but probably built by shepherds as landmarks. The best viewpoints are found at the south end, above the scars.

The path down to Crummack from near Long Scar has changed course since being plotted on Ordnance maps.

Nappa
Scars

The Norber Boulders

Norber is well known far outside its boundaries, at least in geological circles, because of its extensive field of erratic boulders, like a wrecked Stonehenge on a massive scale. On the eastern slope of the hill literally hundreds of huge rock monoliths lie stranded in confusion upon a wide shelf — an amazing scene, one that imparts a feeling of unreality, as though this were not earth but some strange lunar landscape. Fields of boulders are common enough, but this is different. Boulders occur in most hilly districts, usually resulting from erosion of outcrops or the shattering of crags by storms and frost, but some other reason must be sought for the boulders on Norber. These, obviously, have not been caused by collapse of cliffs nor breakup of surface rocks; but transported there. The boulders, of all shapes and sizes, are dark grey in colour but they lie on a bed of white limestone and are, therefore, not native to the place on which they have now come to rest. Certainly they were not brought by man: they serve no purpose and are a hindrance to the farmer.   In fact, they have been moved to their present position, and there abandoned, by the movement of the glacier that once filled Crummack Dale. As it retreated down the valley, at the end of the Ice Age, the hillsides were scoured by the moving ice, loose rocks and low crags being scooped out and pushed along, some being left at the side in the slow process of melting. The source of the Norber boulders can be traced to an area half a mile distant up the valley, and at a slightly lower level, where dark grey rocks of the same 'family' remain in evidence.   Boulders that have, by glacial action, been shifted from their places of origin and deposited in areas of different strata are known as erratics and they occur in most hilly districts, often attracting little attention or being passed unnoticed. But the Norber erratics cannot be disregarded even by the casual and unobservant, for they intrude both on the sight and mind of visitors, and the unlearned perforce learn.

Two of the Norber Boulders

Note that not only does the dark Silurian rock contrast markedly in appearance with the white Carboniferous Limestone, but, being harder and more durable, it has withstood the elements while the softer limestone on which it rests has been worn down by the weather, creating the odd effect that, with the passage of time, the boulders have become suspended on shrinking pedestals of limestone that have survived erosion only by the 'umbrella' protection afforded by the boulders. These pedestals, about 12"-15" high, are therefore a measure of the extent of erosion suffered by the general surface level of the ground since the Ice Age.

WALK 14

from CRUMMACK

8½ miles

INGLEBOROUGH 2373'

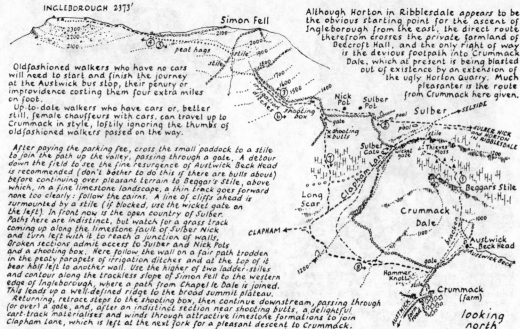

Although Horton in Ribblesdale appears to be the obvious starting point for the ascent of Ingleborough from the east, the direct route therefrom crosses the private farmland of Beecroft Hall, and the only right of way is the devious footpath into Crummack Dale, which at present is being blasted out of existence by an extension of the ugly Horton Quarry. Much pleasanter is the route from Crummack here given.

Oldfashioned walkers who have no cars will need to start and finish the journey at the Austwick bus stop, their penury or improvidence costing them four extra miles on foot.

Up-to-date walkers who have cars or, better still, female chauffeurs with cars, can travel up to Crummack in style, loftily ignoring the thumbs of oldfashioned walkers passed on the way.

After paying the parking fee, cross the small paddock to a stile to join the path up the valley, passing through a gate. A detour down the field to see the fine resurgence of Austwick Beck Head is recommended (don't bother to do this if there are bulls about) before continuing over pleasant terrain to Beggar's stile, above which, in a fine limestone landscape, a thin track goes forward none too clearly: follow the cairns. A line of cliffs ahead is surmounted by a stile (if blocked, use the wicket gate on the left). In front now is the open country of Sulber. Paths here are indistinct, but watch for a grass track coming up along the limestone fault of Sulber Nick and turn left with it to reach a junction of walls. Broken sections admit access to Sulber and Nick Pots and a shooting box. Here follow the wall on a fair path trodden in the peaty parapets of irrigation ditches and at the top of it bear half left to another wall. Use the higher of two ladder-stiles and contour along the trackless slope of Simon Fell to the western edge of Ingleborough, where a path from Chapel le Dale is joined. This leads up a well-defined ridge to the broad summit plateau.

Returning, retrace steps to the shooting box, then continue downstream, passing through (or over) a gate, and, after an indistinct section near shooting butts, a delightful cart-track materialises and winds through attractive limestone formations to join Clapham Lane, which is left at the next fork for a pleasant descent to Crummack.

looking north

MAP

14
(2)

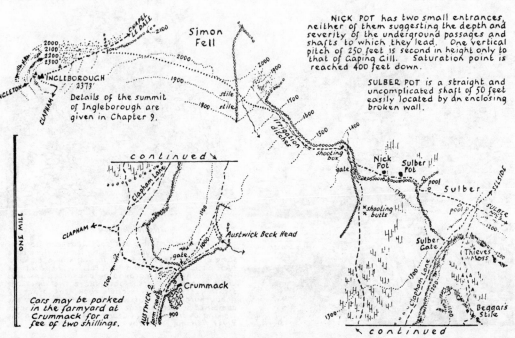

NICK POT has two small entrances, neither of them suggesting the depth and severity of the underground passages and shafts to which they lead. One vertical pitch of 250 feet is second in height only to that of Gaping Gill. Saturation point is reached 400 feet down.

SULBER POT is a straight and uncomplicated shaft of 50 feet easily located by an enclosing broken wall.

Details of the summit of Ingleborough are given in Chapter 9.

Cars may be parked in the farmyard at Crummack for a fee of two shillings.

ONE MILE

continued

continued

Austwick Beck Head

Beggar's Stile

Austwick Beck Head

The streams draining the south-eastern flank of
Simon Fell all sink upon reaching its limestone base,
some of them being engulfed in well-known potholes
such as Juniper Gulf and Nick Pot.   They continue
their journey underground by uncharted passages
until forced to the surface where the limestone
strata rests on impermeable rock, the place of
debouchure being Austwick Beck Head, where the
combined waters emerge from a low cave, thence
flowing overland down Crummack Dale to join the
River Wenning. The cave cannot be entered.

Sulber Pot

Nick Pot

The shooting box

Crummack

THE ASCENT OF MOUGHTON

from WHARFE
(near AUSTWICK)

Moughton is locally pronounced Moot'n

4¼ miles

A delightful ramble with interesting features, *not to be done in mist.*

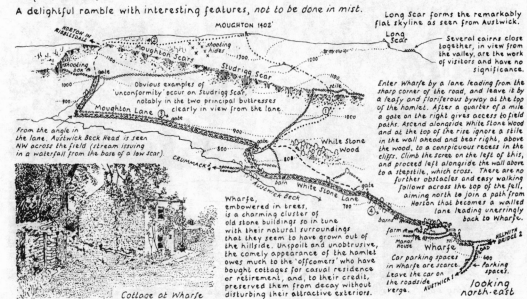

MOUGHTON 1402'

HORTON IN RIBBLESDALE

Moughton Scars

shooting box

shooting Aides

Studrigg Scar

Long Scar

Long Scar forms the remarkable flat skyline as seen from Austwick.

Several cairns close together, in view from the valley, are the work of visitors and have no significance.

Obvious examples of 'unconformity' occur on Studrigg Scar, notably in the two principal buttresses clearly in view from the lane.

Moughton Lane

White Stone Wood

From the angle in the lane, Austwick Beck Head is seen NW across the field (stream issuing in a waterfall from the base of a low scar).

CRUMMACK 1

barn

White Stone Lane

Austwick Beck

Enter Wharfe by a lane leading from the sharp corner of the road, and leave it by a leafy and floriferous byway at the top of the hamlet. After a quarter of a mile a gate on the right gives access to field paths. Ascend alongside White Stone Wood and at the top of the rise ignore a stile in the wall ahead and bear right, above the wood, to a conspicuous recess in the cliffs. Climb the scree on the left of this, and proceed left alongside the wall above to a stepstile, which cross. There are no further obstacles and easy walking follows across the top of the fell, aiming north to join a path from Horton that becomes a walled lane leading unerringly back to Wharfe.

Wharfe, embowered in trees, is a charming cluster of old stone buildings so in tune with their natural surroundings that they seem to have grown out of the hillside. Unspoilt and unobtrusive, the comely appearance of the hamlet owes much to the 'offcomers' who have bought cottages for casual residence or retirement, and, to their credit, preserved them from decay without disturbing their attractive exteriors.

Cottage at Wharfe

farm

Manor House

Wharfe

Car parking spaces in Wharfe are scarce. Leave the car on the roadside verge.

HELWITH BRIDGE 2

Parking spaces.

AUSTWICK 1

looking north-east

Crummack Dale

Cavers and potholers form the largest class of regular visitors to the limestone uplands of Craven, and in second place will probably rank the many parties of students engaged in geological surveys. This is territory with rich rewards for those who come to study its rocks, which lay bare and naked to tell the story of their development through the ages in graphic pictures: hammers and spades are not necessary here to assist in interpretation, the witness of the eyes usually being sufficient. One of the most fruitful of hunting grounds for the geologists is the quiet and isolated valley of Crummack, bounded on the west by Norber, famous for its erratic boulders, and on the east by Moughton, which, apart from its extensive clints, yields many surface evidences of unconformity, exposing to full view the horizontal strata of its limestone cap resting upon the edges of the near-vertical strata of Silurian rocks, a manifestation seen in the escarpment above Crummack Dale and revealed even more conspicuously on the eastern flanks overlooking Ribblesdale, where a few caves add to the interest of exploration.

MAP

HORTON IN RIBBLESDALE 1½

shooting box

Moughton Lane

Moughton Scar

MOUGHTON 1402

Crummack Dale

CRUMMACK

Studrigg Scar

Long Scar

Austwick Beck

White Stone Lane

ONE MILE

Wharfe

AUSTWICK 1

HELWITH BRIDGE 2

The valley floor between Norber and Moughton also exhibits many signs of pressures and folds in the underlying rocks, mainly shales and slates and grits, and higher up the valley, near the old shooting-box on the Horton path, can be found the fine-grained whetstone, identified in the quarry spoil by its red and green bands, that was formerly transported for use in steel manufacture.

There is never a dull moment in and around Crummack Dale for walkers with observant eyes and enquiring minds.

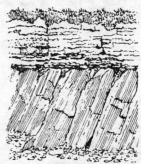

An example of unconformity

Dry waterfall on Moughton. There are now no surface streams on the top of Moughton, but many springs erupt just below the limestone cap. On the west side, a pronounced dip in the escarpment appears to have been caused by water draining from a wide basin behind, but the first evidence of a stream is now found in the scree below. This place is visited on the route of ascent recommended.

Limestone pavement on Moughton. Moughton is predominantly grassy, but large areas of the top of the fell are densely covered by clints, the joints between the stones harbouring grasses and flowers. Walking on these pleasant pavements requires care in placing the feet, especially in wet weather. Limestone is soft, but ankle and leg bones are softer.

The summit of Moughton

The top of Moughton is a pleasant promenade of dry turf interspersed with areas of surface limestone occurring both in extensive clints and isolated outcrops. It is a sheep pasture, bright with flowers in spring and summer. On the north end juniper grows abundantly, and there are tracts of heather and crowberry. An Ordnance Survey column (S 5230) occupies the highest point, which provides an excellent panorama of the nearer Pennines, ranging from the moors around Wensleydale to Pendle Hill in the south. Westwards the Lune and Wenning valleys, with a backing of fells, occupy most of the scene with a picture of gentler beauty.

The ascent should be made in clear weather only, the top being pathless and encircled by a rim of steep cliffs breached by grass slopes that will not be easily located in mist.

THE ENVIRONS OF FEIZOR

from BUCKHAW BROW   *Feizor is pronounced Fayzr*   5 miles

This is a splendid walk in quiet and peaceful surroundings, near the busy A.65 yet a world away. Here is typical limestone country, easy to walk upon, lovely to gaze upon.

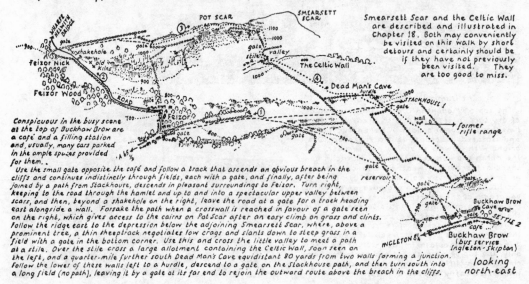

Smearsett Scar and the Celtic Wall are described and illustrated in Chapter 18. Both may conveniently be visited on this walk by short detours and certainly should be if they have not previously been visited. They are too good to miss.

Conspicuous in the busy scene at the top of Buckhaw Brow are a café and a filling station and, usually, many cars parked in the ample spaces provided for them.

Use the small gate opposite the café and follow a track that ascends an obvious breach in the cliffs and continues indistinctly through fields, each with a gate, and finally, after being joined by a path from Stackhouse, descends in pleasant surroundings to Feizor. Turn right, keeping to the road through the hamlet and up to and into a spectacular upper valley between scars, and then, beyond a shakehole on the right, leave the road at a gate for a track heading east alongside a wall. Forsake the path when a crosswall is reached in favour of a gate seen on the right, which gives access to the cairns on Pot Scar after an easy climb on grass and clints. Follow the ridge east to the depression below the adjoining Smearsett Scar, where, above a prominent tree, a thin sheeptrack negotiates low crags and slants down to steep grass in a field with a gate in the bottom corner. Use this and cross the little valley to meet a path at a stile. Over the stile cross a large allotment containing the Celtic Wall, soon seen on the left, and a quarter-mile further south Dead Man's Cave equidistant 80 yards from two walls forming a junction. Follow the lower of these walls left to a hurdle, descend to a gate on the Stackhouse path, and then turn south into a long field (no path), leaving it by a gate at its far end to rejoin the outward route above the breach in the cliffs.

looking north-east

MAP

16
(2)

Buckhaw Brow Cave

Buckhaw Brow Cave is hidden from sight by trees at the base of the escarpment overlooking the road. It will be found up the slope about 80 yards to the right of the wicket-gate opposite the café. Its unusual arrangement, consisting of two levels connected by a rock chute, is ascribed to mining operations, but the shortness of the passages and the absence of debris (other than the tin cans left behind by the scruffy devils who have used the cave as free lodgings) suggest that it was not very productive. The higher level is 15 feet long, the lower is a tight crawl amidst the remains of meals for 60 feet.

Caves are usually sited in hollows or stream channels slightly below general ground level, or at the foot of scars.

Dead Man's Cave is out of the rut, occupying a vantage point on the brow of a hillside. It is one of the few caves with an extensive view from its entrance.

The higher level

On the return journey a curious wall in the penultimate field (last but one, children) is a puzzling feature: crescent-shaped in plan, and about 50 yards long, it stands in isolation. It is fairly modern, with coping stones, and therefore not another Celtic Wall. It is not an enclosure and so cannot be a sheepfold. It is too high and too elaborate for a bield. Possibly it served as the target wall for a former rifle range? (LATER NOTE: Yes, it did)

The Ordnance Survey spell Buckhaw as two words, Buck Haw. Everybody locally knows it as Bucka.

Feizor Nick
Smakehole
LITTLE STAINFORTH 1½
Feizor Wood
POT SCAR
SMEARSETT SCAR
AUSTWICK 1½ (lane)
Feizor
FEIZOR
LITTLE STAINFORTH ¾
A.65 ½
The Celtic Wall
STACKHOUSE 1¼
Dead Man's Cave
STACKHOUSE ¾
wall
ONE MILE
INGLETON 8½
ROAD
Buckhaw Brow Cave
Buckhaw Brow
café
SETTLE 2
A.65

Feizor

Feizor has paid lip-service to progress by having its only road surfaced, but prefers to retain the two gates and cobbled watersplash across it. This is a shy hamlet, nestling in a wooded hollow and hidden on all sides from the eyes of passing travellers. It is shy, not because it lacks charm, but because it clings to the quiet life it has always known. Few will visit it and not be envious.

In this land of disappearing streams, despite a rainfall above average, water is a scarce commodity. Examples can be seen in the district of man-made channels to convey streams overland across the limestone: in Feizor a community pump and rainwater tanks augment supplies. The pump, clean as a new pin, stands on a trim and tidy green as a thing of pride and joy, and for sentiment's sake one hopes it will never be demolished, or dismantled and taken to an urban museum. It typifies Feizor.

left: *The summit of Pot Scar*

Pot Scar, a lofty steep-fronted 'headland' liberally decorated with naked limestone, has a vast mound of loose stones on its crest like a tumulus, from which two modern cairns have sprouted. It is a fine viewpoint, extensive in all directions, with Feizor seen below.

below: *Dead Man's Cave*

This roomy cave, 8 yards long, is an excellent shelter and can be entered without difficulty.
There are no dead men in it......... At least, there weren't on 2nd. Sept 1968.

GIGGLESWICK SCAR

from GIGGLESWICK   4½ miles

Overlooking the A.65, yet remote from its noise and bustle, Giggleswick Scar provides a simple and beautiful high-level traverse, abounding in interesting situations and splendid viewpoints.

Schoolboys Tower gets its name from an old tradition requiring new boys at Giggleswick School each to add a stone to the cairn.

From the edge of the quarry the path, still descending, circles north to a gate at the far end of Lord's Wood. An overgrown lane leads to a field, at the far corner of which either join the Stackhouse road nearby or preferably bear right along a rising tree-lined drive and so reach the village through a recently-developed residential estate.

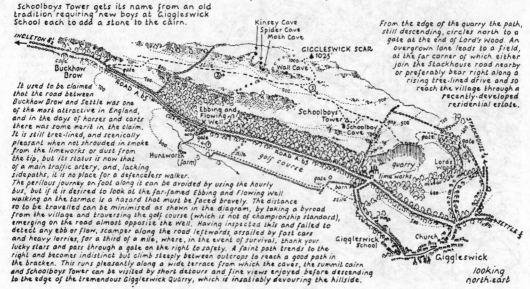

It used to be claimed that the road between Buckhaw Brow and Settle was one of the most attractive in England, and in the days of horses and carts there was some merit in the claim. It is still tree-lined, and scenically pleasant when not shrouded in smoke from the limeworks or dust from the tip, but its status is now that of a main traffic artery, and, lacking sidepaths, it is no place for a defenceless walker. The perilous journey on foot along it can be avoided by using the hourly bus, but if it is desired to look at the far-famed Ebbing and Flowing Well walking on the tarmac is a hazard that must be faced bravely. The distance so to be travelled can be minimised as shown in the diagram, by taking a byroad from the village and traversing the golf course (which is not of championship standard), emerging on the road almost opposite the Well. Having inspected this and failed to detect any ebb or flow, scamper along the road leftwards, assailed by fast cars and heavy lorries, for a third of a mile, where, in the event of survival, thank your lucky stars and pass through a gate on the right to safety. A faint path trends to the right and becomes indistinct but climb steeply between outcrops to reach a good path in the bracken. This runs pleasantly along a wide terrace from which the caves, the summit cairn and Schoolboys Tower can be visited by short detours and fine views enjoyed before descending to the edge of the tremendous Giggleswick Quarry, which is insatiably devouring the hillside.

looking north-east

MAP

ONE MILE

The shallow valley of Huntworth Beck once contained a tarn. This was drained in 1837 and subsequent excavations brought to light a canoe 2000 years old.

The Ebbing and Flowing Well

A unique phenomenon that aroused much interest and speculation in years gone by, before there was space travel to marvel at, was the rise and fall of water in this elaborate roadside well, caused by an underground syphon in the rocks below. In its heyday, much was written about it, both in prose and verse. But today its performances are decidedly meagre and the few people who have witnessed the ebb and flow are themselves becoming unique, while those who have watched the well for hours without anything happening are numbered in legions.

Caves numbered on the map:
1: Kinsey Cave
2: Spider Cave
3: Moth Cave
4: Wall Cave
5: Schoolboy Cave

These caves may conveniently be visited on the walk, being easily accessible and near to the route, but Wall Cave is the only one clearly in view from the path.

Kinsey Cave, behind elder bushes at the head of a side-valley, has yielded many interesting finds including the skull of a bear.

Spider Cave is found at the head of the next side-valley, above a scree slope; it has a low entrance.

Moth Cave, around the corner of the cliff from Spider Cave, facing the path, is partially blocked.

Wall Cave, facing the path and conspicuous, has a stone wall across its entrance. A feature is the admission of daylight through two holes in the roof.

Schoolboy Cave burrows under Schoolboys Tower, the entrance being only 20 yards from the big cairn.

All these caves occur at the base of low scars and can safely be inspected. None exceeds 100 feet in length. Don't wear your Sunday best.

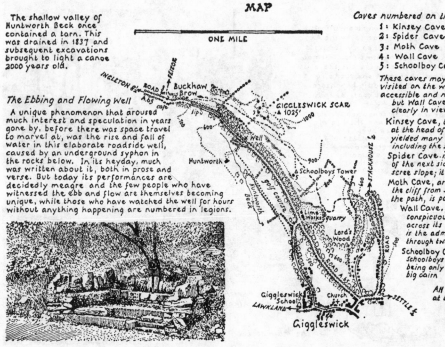

INGLETON 8½
ROAD
PATROW
A.65 car
Buckhaw Brow
1150
GIGGLESWICK SCAR
1025'
1000
600
Well
600
Huntworth
900
Schoolboys Tower
5
STACKHOUSE LANE
Golf course
Huntworth Beck
Lime Works
Quarry
600
Lord's Wood
ROAD A.65
Giggleswick School
LAWKLAND
Church
SETTLE 1½
Giggleswick

Giggleswick

The village of Giggleswick, mentioned in the Domesday Book, is, happily, bypassed by the A.65, and its picturesque old-world beauty suggests that it has been bypassed by time too. Tarmac has replaced cobbles in the street but there is little else of recent change in the scene, and quaint buildings and alleys huddle haphazardly around the church and market cross as they have done for centuries.

Giggleswick has long been renowned for its public school, founded in 1507, and the life of the village is greatly influenced by it. The present establishment is accommodated in handsome buildings, and the green-domed school chapel is a well-known landmark. It gained national prominence on the occasion of the 1927 eclipse, being the official observation point of the Astronomer Royal and his staff.

Industry at Giggleswick

the lime works

the quarry

The Parish Church
(St. Alkelda's)

The main street

Giggleswick Scar

Travellers along the road from Kirkby Lonsdale to Settle follow the line of a major geological fault. On their left is the distinctive scenery of the limestone uplands; on their right is flat pastureland, pleasant but unexciting. At many points on the left the characteristic white scars and terraces can be clearly seen against a dark background of moors. Yet, apart from the stark outline of Ingleborough, the contrast in terrain between left and right may not be noticed particularly—until the crest of Buckhaw Brow is reached. There, suddenly, a striking scene is revealed, the ground ahead erupting into a rising wave of tiered limestone cliffs with the road descending sharply to run along its wooded base and bordering a dreary flatland of gritstone shales. The metamorphosis is palpably clear. Something dramatic once happened to the earth in the place now known as Giggleswick Scar.

Kinsey Cave

Wall Cave

looking to Ingleborough

Views from the summit

looking to Penyghent

Schoolboys Tower

Schoolboy Cave

Penyghent and Stackhouse, from near Lord's Wood

THE CELTIC WALL AND SMEARSETT SCAR

from STACKHOUSE

5 miles

Pot Scar

SMEARSETT SCAR
1193'

Smearsett Scar, so named on Ordnance maps, is better known locally as Smearside.

Little Stainforth is also known as Knight Stainforth.

Little Stainforth Hall
STAINFORTH
(not for cars)

FEIZOR

The Celtic Wall

The Happy Valley

limekiln

earthworks

gate
stile
gate
gap
pond
stile
gap

Stainforth Lane

The return to Stackhouse may be made by road, or preferably, as here shown, by a field-path leaving the road at a stile near a boundary stone (Giggleswick – Stainforth): there is no clear path but stiles and gates indicate the way.

Two lanes enter Stackhouse from the road. Use the northerly one and persist to its end as a walled passage emerging on the wooded hillside. Climb the slope ahead to a stile in a crosswall and continue over the next field to a gate, beyond which a path to Feizor ascends half-left. But go alongside the wall on the right, using well-trodden gaps in crosswalls to reach an old lane where a high and awkward stile admits to a thistly field. Now proceed along the well-defined valley ahead between parallel limestone scars fringed with trees ('The Happy Valley'). At its head is a gate, with Smearsett Scar now fully in view. The Celtic Wall is out of sight on the little escarpment on the left above a broken wall, and is unmistakable when reached: a thrilling moment for the imaginative visitor! To ascend Smearsett Scar, cross the valley, rounding the walls on the left to a wicket-gate and a steep grass slope: a sheep-track trending left is a help in negotiating the scars above. At a prominent tree turn right along the ridge to the summit, noting from this height the Celtic Wall, now clearly seen especially when shadowed by the sun, and the ridged lines of the earthworks of an old encampment in the valley bottom. Leave the summit by its easier north-east slope, circling right to return to the valley alongside a wall that can be scaled at a tumbled corner where a stile would be of better service. Now look for an authentic crossing of the wall, around the corner on the left, carrying a route going down to Little Stainforth, the path being indistinct initially but improving when the hamlet comes into sight and becoming a stony lane.

FEIZOR

Reinber Scar
barn

Hanging Scar

STACKHOUSE ROAD
SETTLE ROAD

Stackhouse

LANGCLIFFE
(not for cars)

looking north-east

A delectable expedition for a sunny summer's day; a joyous outing.

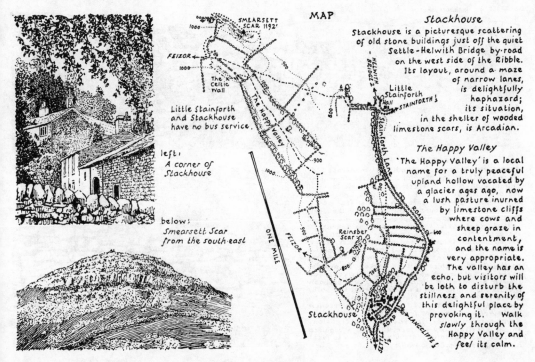

MAP

Stackhouse

Stackhouse is a picturesque scattering of old stone buildings just off the quiet Settle - Helwith Bridge by-road on the west side of the Ribble. Its layout, around a maze of narrow lanes, is delightfully haphazard; its situation, in the shelter of wooded limestone scars, is Arcadian.

The Happy Valley

'The Happy Valley' is a local name for a truly peaceful upland hollow vacated by a glacier ages ago, now a lush pasture inurned by limestone cliffs where cows and sheep graze in contentment, and the name is very appropriate. The valley has an echo, but visitors will be loth to disturb the stillness and serenity of this delightful place by provoking it. Walk *slowly* through the Happy Valley and *feel* its calm.

SMEARSETT SCAR 1192'

FEIZOR ←

The X Celtic Wall

Little Stainforth and Stackhouse have no bus service.

left: A corner of Stackhouse

below: Smearsett Scar from the south-east

HELWITH BRIDGE 2

Little Stainforth Hall

STAINFORTH ½

Stainforth Lane

The Happy Valley

ONE MILE

FEIZOR ←

Reinsber Scar

ROAD

Stackhouse

SETTLE ROAD

LANGCLIFFE ½

Ingleborough

Simon Fell

Smearsett Scar

Pot Scar

The Celtic Wall

Across the shallow valley south of Smearsett Scar
there stands, on the brow of a small escarpment, an
antiquity of unique interest: a strong limestone wall
approximately 65' in length, 5' in height, and 5' wide
at the base. (60 yards east is a smaller fragment of
wall with adjacent foundations from which the stones
have been removed). The appearance of the wall, at
first glance, suggests that it was built as a shelter for
sheep, such structures being common in the district,
but its unusual thickness and obvious age support a
conjecture that its purpose was that of a defensive
shield for an ancient encampment in the valley, the
earthworks of which can still be traced. Excavation
of the sites of similar walls, however, has revealed
them to be places of burial, and this was probably
the use here. The wall is not seen from the paths
in the vicinity and stands in lonely isolation on an
elevated and unfrequented pasture, its remoteness
(and surprising omission from Ordnance maps) no
doubt accounting for its excellent preservation.
This interesting survival from the past, thought to
be over two thousand years old, is known to local
historians as the Celtic Wall.

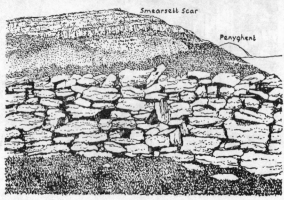

Smearsett Scar

Penyghent

The west ridge
Smearsett Scar

Smearsett Scar

The triangle of upland country lying between Helwith Bridge, Feizor and Giggleswick forms a pleasant succession of limestone scars and green valleys threaded by enchanting grass paths — a quiet and charming territory for the discerning walker. The area is dominated by the abrupt upthrust of Smearsett Scar, which, although of modest elevation, yet contrives a spectacular outline, especially when seen in profile from the vicinity of Stainforth.

The summit, topping the tiered south face, is a fine viewpoint, its isolated position permitting excellent panoramas, especially extensive west and south. The large heap of stones here, from which a few cairns have been fashioned may, it is thought, be the debris of a former watch-tower. There is less room for doubt about the origin of a cemented column nearby, numbered S. 5449.

The summit

Stainforth Hall

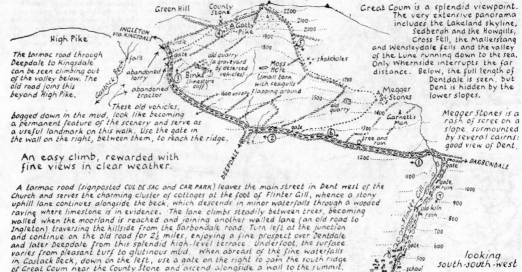

Great Coum is a splendid viewpoint. The very extensive panorama includes the Lakeland skyline, Sedbergh and the Howgills, Cross Fell, the Mallerstang and Wensleydale fells, and the valley of the Lune running down to the sea. Only Whernside interrupts the far distance. Below, the full length of Dentdale is seen, but Dent is hidden by the lower slopes.

The tarmac road through Deepdale to Kingsdale can be seen climbing out of the valley below. The old road joins this beyond High Pike.

These old vehicles, bogged down in the mud, look like becoming a permanent feature of the scenery and serve as a useful landmark on this walk. Use the gate in the wall on the right, between them, to reach the ridge.

Megger Stones is a rash of scree on a slope, surmounted by several cairns: good view of Dent.

An easy climb, rewarded with fine views in clear weather.

A tarmac road (signposted CUL DE SAC and CAR PARK) leaves the main street in Dent west of the Church and serves the charming cluster of cottages at the foot of Flinter Gill, whence a stony uphill lane continues alongside the beck, which descends in minor waterfalls through a wooded ravine where limestone is in evidence. The lane climbs steadily between trees, becoming walled when the moorland is reached and joining another walled lane (an old road to Ingleton) traversing the hillside from the Barbondale road. Turn left at the junction and continue on the old road for 2½ miles, enjoying a fine prospect over Dentdale and later Deepdale from this splendid high-level terrace. Underfoot, the surface varies from pleasant turf to glutinous mud. When abreast of the fine waterfalls in Gastack Beck, down on the left, use a gate on the right to gain the south ridge of Great Coum near the County Stone and ascend alongside a wall to the summit. Crosswalls have to be climbed in the absence of stiles but are not difficult.
Leave the summit by following the wall going down in the direction of Dentdale and when it turns to descend to the old road keep on ahead to see the Megger Stones before doing likewise. Thenceforward the route of ascent is reversed and charming Flinter Gill visited again.

looking south-south-west

MAP

19
(2)

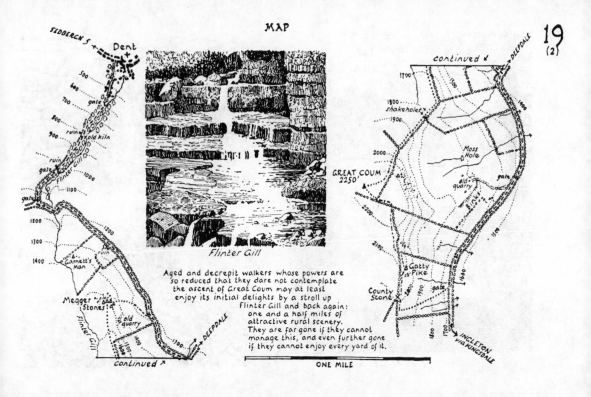

Flinter Gill

SEDBERGH 5

Dent

500
600   gate
700
800
900   ruin of old kiln
ruin
gate   Flinter Gill
1000
1100
gate
1200
1300
1400   Garnett's
Man
ruin
1200

Megger
Stones
old
quarry
Flinter Gill
1500
1600
1300   DEEPDALE

continued ↗

DEEPDALE
continued ↙

1700
1800
1900   sinkholes
1900
2000   Moss
Hole
GREAT COUM
2250'
old
quarry
gate
Twin
Blaks
2200
2100
Gatty
Pike
County
Stone
gate
1900
1800
1700
1800   INGLETON
VIA KINGSDALE

Aged and decrepit walkers whose powers are
so reduced that they dare not contemplate
the ascent of Great Coum may at least
enjoy its initial delights by a stroll up
Flinter Gill and back again:
one and a half miles of
attractive rural scenery.
They are far gone if they cannot
manage this, and even further gone
if they cannot enjoy every yard of it.

ONE MILE

The road to Flinter Gill

The County Stone

Cairn on
Gatty Pike

Summit cairn,
Great Coum

Cairns at Megger Stones

HELL'S CAULDRON AND IBBETH PERIL

via GIBB'S HALL ; returning via WHERNSIDE MANOR

6 miles

Although largely a road-walk, this simple tour of mid-Dentdale is an excellent introduction to the delights of the valley, being consistently pleasant and affording lovely views. There is little traffic to disturb enjoyment of the scenery.

A feature of Dentdale is the remarkable number of farmhouses, cottages and barns on the lower slopes of the fells on both sides of the valley. No other Yorkshire dale can boast such intensive husbandry, mile for mile, nor a fairer prospect.

[map labels:] HAWES 11½ · ROAD · River Dee · footbridge · Gibb's Hall · IBBETH PERIL · ROAD · 700 · gate · cave · Nacker Gill · stile · Hackergill Bridge · Hell's Cauldron · lower slopes of Whernside · footbridge · Cross House · lower slopes of Rise Hill · 600 · 500 · Tommy Bridge · footbridge · Tub Hole · 600 · ford · old kiln · Woman's Land · 500 · Scotchergill Bridge · SEDBERGH 5 · River Dee · 500 · Church Bridge · Dent · Field Beck · Double Croft · Deepdale Beck · Whernside Manor · DEEPDALE · looking east·north·east · Mill Bridge · chapel · ROAD · DENT 1¼ (road) · 500

GIBB'S HALL, now a sad ruin, was once a literary centre of Dentdale, being the home of William Howitt ('Rural Life of England') and his wife Mary ('Hope on, hope ever'). On Ordnance maps the name is spelt *Gib's Hall*.

IBBETH PERIL, also known as Ibby Peril, is the haunt of a witch. A cave here penetrates deep into the limestone.

HELL'S CAULDRON is also known as Hell Cauldron.

WHERNSIDE MANOR, a fine Georgian house in wooded grounds, and once the home of the Mason family (ironstone pottery fame) is today in the occupation of the National Scout Caving Activity Centre.

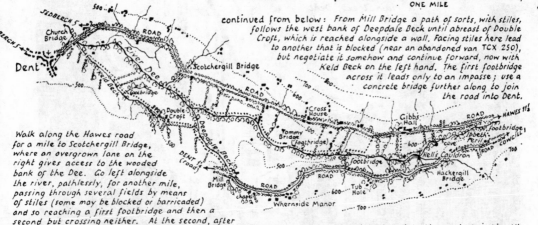

continued from below: From Mill Bridge a path of sorts, with stiles, follows the west bank of Deepdale Beck until abreast of Double Croft, which is reached alongside a wall. Facing stiles here lead to another that is blocked (near an abandoned van TCX 250), but negotiate it somehow and continue forward, now with Keld Beck on the left hand. The first footbridge across it leads only to an impasse; use a concrete bridge further along to join the road into Dent.

Walk along the Hawes road for a mile to Scotchergill Bridge, where an overgrown lane on the right gives access to the wooded bank of the Dee. Go left alongside the river, pathlessly, for another mile, passing through several fields by means of stiles (some may be blocked or barricaded) and so reaching a first footbridge and then a second but crossing neither. At the second, after looking at the interesting limestone formations in the river bed, turn up the field to rejoin the road at a thin stile. (There is a doubt whether this detour by the riverside is a right of way, although the stiles suggest it is and the Ordnance maps indicate it as a footpath. It can, of course, be omitted by keeping to the road throughout). At Gibb's Hall ask permission at the farm to visit Hell's Cauldron, and, having obtained it, go down the field towards the river, here flowing in a deep ravine. At a stile in a fence a path leads steeply down to the stony bed, and this can be followed upstream to the waterfall. Return to the road the same way, but detour along the fence to the left, above the ravine, to see Hacker Gill cascading into the Dee. (200 yards upstream, an underground channel of Hacker Gill emerges from a cave). A half-mile further, near the roadside but densely screened by trees, is Ibbeth Peril, a force at the head of the ravine; to see it, step down at the end of a short wall bounding the road. Just beyond, an open space at the roadside is crossed to a footbridge giving access to a field and a narrow by-road along which a pleasant return to Dent may be made. Or, at Mill Bridge, a field path may be taken, in which case see the note above.

Main Street, Dent

Hell's Cauldron

Ibbeth Peril

from DENT : 10½ miles

This is a fine walk on a fine day,
with excellent views. Although
somewhat tedious underfoot
it is the best of all routes
up Whernside because of
the lovely countryside
from which it springs.

Walkers with cars can save 3 miles
road-walking by motoring to the
Methodist Chapel and parking
their cars there.
If this is done, an
alternative way
back to the chapel
is by a footpath
(much overgrown)
from Outrake
foot, crossing
Deepdale Beck
by footbridge
as shown in
the diagram.

Leave the summit at a right angle
to the wall, descending west to
join a wall coming in from the right.
This points the way down to the
Ingleton road, which is then used
for the return to Dent via Deepdale.
Tarmac-haters will prefer the old lane
and reach Dent via Flinter Gill.

looking east

Leave Dent by the street alongside the George and Dragon and the Post
Office : it is not signposted, through traffic being discouraged, although
it is the only road access to the populated side-valley of Deepdale and continues to
Ingleton by the shortest and most spectacular route. On the outward journey follow
the road beyond the Ingleton junction to Deepdale Methodist Chapel. Here turn up a side-road
to a lane on the left, where an old path to Ribblehead once known as Cravens Way starts its
long climb over the shoulder of Whernside. When, at 1650', this path breaks clear of walls and
reaches open country turn right and ascend to the two prominent cairns on Pike. Now head
south, gradually rising and soon passing the surprising Whernside Tarns, to cross the wall ahead
where it is joined by another broken one coming up on the left. The summit, still distant, is
reached unerringly simply by following a wall upwards along the ridge.

The summit of Whernside, looking to Ingleborough

For a MAP of the journey see the next two pages ⟶

Lockin Garth Force

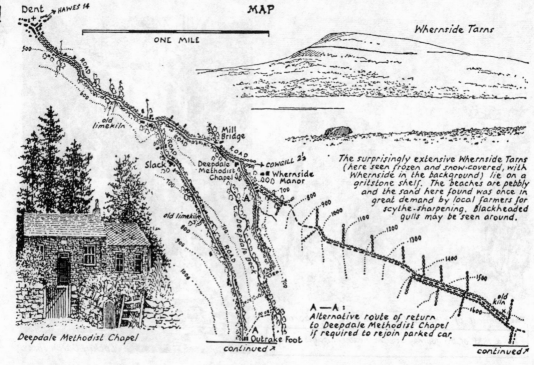

Dent → HAWES 14

MAP

ONE MILE

Whernside Tarns

500

ROAD

800

old limekiln

ROAD

Mill Bridge

ROAD

Slack

Deepdale Methodist Chapel

→ COWGILL 2½

Whernside Manor

A

700

old limekiln

700

800

Deepdale Beck

900

1000

The surprisingly extensive Whernside Tarns (here seen frozen and snow-covered, with Whernside in the background) lie on a gritstone shelf. The beaches are pebbly and the sand here found was once in great demand by local farmers for scythe-sharpening. Blackheaded gulls may be seen around.

800

900

1000

1100

1200

1300

1400

1500

old kiln

1600

A — A :
Alternative route of return to Deepdale Methodist Chapel if required to rejoin parked car.

Deepdale Methodist Chapel

A
Outrake Foot

continued ↗

continued ↗

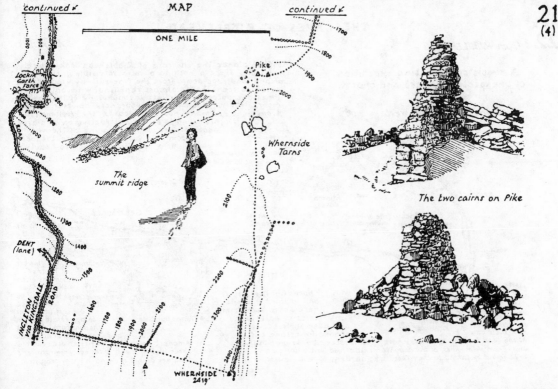

MAP

21
(4)

continued ↙

continued ↙

ONE MILE

1700
1800
1900
2000

Pike
△ △

Lockin
Garth
Force
1175

800
900
ruin
1000
ROAD
1100

The
summit ridge

Whernside
Tarns

1200

1300

DENT
(lane)

1400

1500

2100

INGLETON VIA KINGSDALE
ROAD

1600 1700 1800 1900 2000 2100

2200

2300

2400

WHERNSIDE
2419'

The two cairns on Pike

A simple cave-hunting expedition of unexpected interest and charm.

At first glance the environs of Ribblehead look entirely unpromising. There is nothing of interest visible in the bleak moorland landscape apart from the fine railway viaduct, the desolate scene being almost repelling, with only a few limestone outcrops to relieve the monotony of the sombre moor. Never judge on first appearances, however. Hidden from sight are many interesting caves; the limestone scars are found to be very attractive on a closer acquaintance, and the ravine of Thorns Gill, completely unsuspected from the road, is a paradise of exquisite beauty.

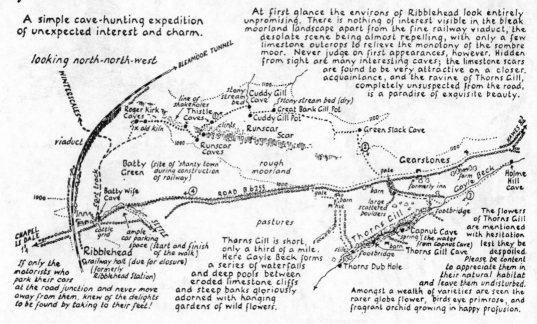

looking north-north-west

BLEAMOOR TUNNEL

WINTERSCALES

line of shakeholes
Roger Kirk Caves
Thistle Caves
x old kiln
clints
Runscar Caves
Runscar Scar
stony stream bed
Cuddy Gill Cave
stony stream bed (dry)
Great Bank Gill Pol
Cuddy Gill Pol
Green Slack Cave

viaduct

Batty Green (site of 'shanty town' during construction of railway)

rough moorland

Gearstones

gate
O...O farm (formerly inn)
Gayle Beck
Holme Hill Cave

HAWES 8¼

Batty Wife Cave

1000

ROAD B.6255
1000

gate
barn
barn hut
barn
large scattered boulders
footbridge

pastures

Thorns Gill

CHAPEL LE DALE 1¼

Inn
cattle grid
ample car parking space (start and finish of the walk)

Ribblehead
Railway halt (due for closure) (formerly Ribblehead Station)

Thorns Gill is short, only a third of a mile. Here Gayle Beck forms a series of waterfalls and deep pools between eroded limestone cliffs and steep banks gloriously adorned with hanging gardens of wild flowers.

stile
footbridge
Capnut Cave
spring (the water from Capnut Cave)
Thorns Gill Cave
barn
Thorns Dub Hole

footbridge

If only the motorists who park their cars at the road junction and never move away from them, knew of the delights to be found by taking to their feet!

The flowers of Thorns Gill are mentioned with hesitation lest they be despoiled. Please be content to appreciate them in their natural habitat and leave them undisturbed. Amongst a wealth of varieties are seen the rarer globe flower, birds eye primrose, and fragrant orchid growing in happy profusion.

MAP

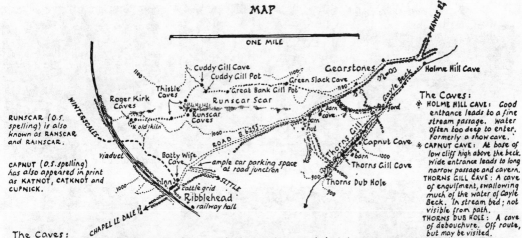

ONE MILE

RUNSCAR (O.S. spelling) is also known as RANSCAR and RAINSCAR.

CAPNUT (O.S. spelling) has also appeared in print as KATNOT, CATKNOT and CUPNICK.

The Caves:

* **HOLME HILL CAVE:** Good entrance leads to a fine stream passage. Water often too deep to enter. Formerly a show cave.
* **CAPNUT CAVE:** At base of low cliff high above the beck. Wide entrance leads to long narrow passage and cavern.

THORNS GILL CAVE: A cave of engulfment, swallowing much of the water of Gayle Beck. In stream bed; not visible from path.

THORNS DUB HOLE: A cave of debouchure. Off route, but may be visited.

The Caves:

BATTY WIFE CAVE: At the roadside below the inn, where the cart track turns off. A simple low passage. Stream normally emerges.

ROGER KIRK CAVES: Main entrance near old kiln, facing viaduct, where small stream emerges. Second entrance in shakehole 40 yards east.

THISTLE CAVES: (1) Small entrance amongst rocks in deep shakehole. Interesting cluster of miniature stalactites seen by looking in.
(2) Hole (covered) at base of large rock in shakehole on the edge of the clints on top of Runscar Scar.

RUNSCAR CAVES: Four ways in amongst huge fallen blocks in a depression at the west end of Runscar Scar. Stream below surface. In the next depression 40 yards south are two more entrances, one of them imposing, with underground stream clearly visible.

* **CUDDY GILL CAVE:** Main entrance at end of stony stream channel. Second entrance 10 yards away through natural archway.

CUDDY GILL POT: The only surface pothole on the moor. 30 feet deep. Easily descended at the east side. Fringed with trees. Rich in flowers.

GREAT BANK GILL POT: Small hole in peat bank at end of dry stream bed. Unimpressive. A complete contrast to Cuddy Gill Pot.

GREEN SLACK CAVE: Small entrance in shakehole amongst limestone outcrops, situated in a shallow valley on the moor.

There is often more fun in locating caves than in exploring their interiors. Caves are dirty and spidery, usually dripping wet, sometimes dangerous, and, of course, dark. Intrepid novices who don't care a damn about their clothes will find the three caves marked ✳ interesting, easy to enter and safe to follow until their nerves break under the strain.

Batty Wife Cave

↑ Entrances to Runscar Caves ↓

Cuddy Gill Cave

Roger Kirk Cave

Limestone boulder perched on
limestone pedestal, Thorns Gill.

a pool in
Thorns Gill

Capnut Cave

footbridge, Thorns Gill

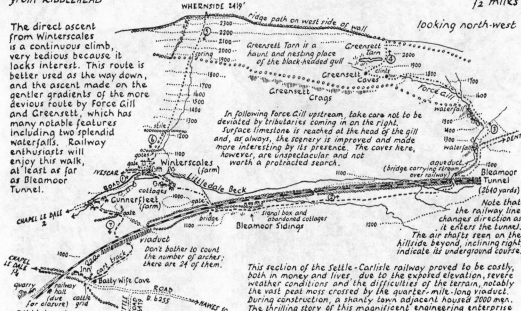

The direct ascent from Winterscales is a continuous climb, very tedious because it lacks interest. This route is better used as the way down, and the ascent made on the gentler gradients of the more devious route by Force Gill and Greensett, which has many notable features including two splendid waterfalls. Railway enthusiasts will enjoy this walk, at least as far as Bleamoor Tunnel.

WHERNSIDE 2419'

ridge path on west side of wall

Greensett Tarn is a haunt and nesting place of the black-headed gull

Greensett Tarn

Greensett Caves

Greensett Crags

Force Gill

waterfall

In following Force Gill upstream, take care not to be deviated by tributaries coming in on the right.
Surface limestone is reached at the head of the gill and, as always, the scenery is improved and made more interesting by its presence. The caves here, however, are unspectacular and not worth a protracted search.

DENT

waterfall

spring

stile

gate

gate

Winterscales (farm)

IVESCAR ROAD

Littledale Beck

cottages

Gunnerfleet (farm)

gate

gate

bridge

signal box and abandoned cottages

Bleamoor Sidings

aqueduct
(bridge carrying stream over railway)

Bleamoor Tunnel
(2640 yards)

Note that the railway line changes direction as it enters the tunnel. The air shafts seen on the hillside beyond, inclining right, indicate its underground course.

CHAPEL LE DALE 2

CHAPEL LE DALE 1¼

quarry

railway halt (due for closure)

Inn

cart track

Batty Wife Cave

cattle grid

viaduct

Don't bother to count the number of arches; there are 24 of them.

ROAD B.6255

SETTLE ROAD B.6479

HAWES 10

Ribblehead

This section of the Settle-Carlisle railway proved to be costly, both in money and lives, due to the exposed elevation, severe weather conditions and the difficulties of the terrain, notably the vast peat moss crossed by the quarter-mile-long viaduct. During construction, a shanty town adjacent housed 2000 men. The thrilling story of this magnificent engineering enterprise has been well told in several books.

MAP

23
(2)

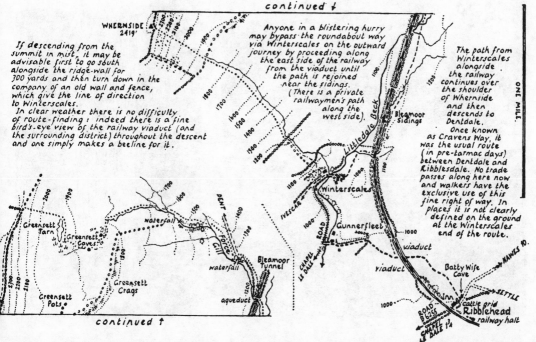

continued ↑

WHERNSIDE
2419'

If descending from the summit in mist, it may be advisable first to go south alongside the ridge-wall for 300 yards and then turn down in the company of an old wall and fence, which give the line of direction to Winterscales.

In clear weather there is no difficulty of route-finding : indeed there is a fine bird's-eye view of the railway viaduct (and the surrounding district) throughout the descent and one simply makes a beeline for it.

Anyone in a blistering hurry may bypass the roundabout way via Winterscales on the outward journey by proceeding along the east side of the railway from the viaduct until the path is rejoined near the sidings.
(There is a private railwaymen's path along the west side).

The path from Winterscales alongside the railway continues over the shoulder of Whernside and then descends to Dentdale.

Once known as Cravens Way, it was the usual route (in pre-tarmac days) between Dentdale and Ribblesdale. No trade passes along here now and walkers have the exclusive use of this fine right of way. In places it is not clearly defined on the ground at the Winterscales end of the route.

ONE MILE.

Littledale Beck

Bleamoor Sidings

Winterscales

IVESCALE

ROAD

Gunnerfleet

Greensett Tarn

Greensett Caves

waterfall

DENT FELL
GILL

waterfall

Bleamoor Tunnel

CHAPEL LE DALE

aqueduct

viaduct

viaduct

Batty Wife Cave

HAWES 10.

Greensett Crags

Greensett Pots

Inn

cattle grid

Ribblehead

railway halt

SETTLE

ROAD B 6255

CHAPEL LE DALE 1¾

continued ↓

Winterscales

Bleamoor Tunnel

Force Gill

the lower fall

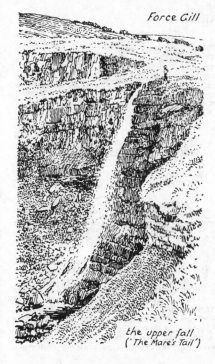

Force Gill

the upper fall
('The Mare's Tail')

Upper Greensett Cave

Greensett Tarn

WHERNSIDE

Between Ellerbeck and Winterscales the path is indicated by a succession of gates (too numerous to be shown individually on this diagram). These gates are a useful guide, the path itself being indistinct in places. The route in this section runs along the base of a wooded limestone scar with little rise or fall.

2400
2300
2200
2100
2000
1900
1800
1700
1600
1500
1400
1300
1200
1100
1000

Winterscales *(farm)*

Ivescar *(farm)*

Ellerbeck *(farm)*

Hodge Hole *(byre)*

Bruntscar *(farm)*

Broadrake *(farm)*

Scar Top

caves

old limekiln

cave

Scar Top Waterfall

Gunnerfleet *(farm)*

barn

kingcups in profusion

farm road

ruin

ROAD

Winterscales Beck

ford

limestone outcrops

cattle grid

Gill Head

pastures

cross dry stream bed

barn

Gatekirk Cave

gates

The detour to Gatekirk Cave is more clearly seen on the map opposite. SEE NOTE.

looking north-north-west

There are no bus services to Chapel le Dale.

Weathercote House Cave

HIGH SCALES

cattle grids

school

Philpin *(farm)*

ROAD B 6255

HAWES 11¾

Hill Inn

SOUTHER SCALES

Lying parallel to the Chapel le Dale – Ribblehead road, and a mile distant therefrom, is a low limestone scar bedecked with an array of trees and sheltering a line of farmsteads. It provides a simple walk, everywhere interesting and in some respects unique, and is especially delightful in summer, when the pastures are rich in flowers. The way thereto, visiting Weathercote, is entirely charming.

Hurtle Pot

Church

Chapel-le-Dale

INGLETON 4

MAP

24
(2)

The outward journey:

Go down the road from the Hill Inn for 300 yards, passing the school, and enter a gate on the right, whence a path leads alongside a fence to Weathercote, delightfully situated in a hollow. The cave (better described as a pothole) is enclosed by a wall, access being gained by a gate (key at the house: 6d): it is an awesome and spectacular hole, shaded by trees, into which a waterfall pours, and rough steps lead down under a rock bridge into its gloomy depths. Suitably impressed, return the key and proceed south along a cart-track by a wall, over which there is a glimpse of Jingle Pot. At the end of the wall turn sharp right to cross the dry stream bed and look at Hurtle Pot (fenced). A pleasant lane skirts the top of this fearful abyss and is followed uphill past a neat signpost, with Weathercote now down on the right, to the charming old house of Gill Head, the way lying through a flowery dell. From the end of the walled lane beyond Gill Head Ellerbeck is seen ahead, and, now in open country with fine views, the general line of the route to be followed, along the base of Whernside, is clear.

ONE MILE

Winterscales

caves

Scar Top

Ivescar

Gunnerfleet

ROAD

RIBBLEHEAD

Scar Top Waterfall

Winterscale Beck

WHERNSIDE

1100

Broadrake

Bruntscar cave

1100

Gatekirk Cave

Hodge Hole

1100

ROAD

The return journey:

A tarmac road links Winterscales with the B6255 above the Hill Inn. Follow this road for a mile until a wooded glen appears on the right. Gatekirk Cave lies amongst the trees, in beautiful river scenery. To reach it, leave the road and use a gate away to the right in a wall, then crossing an enclosing fence. The cave may be entered, the awkward low entrance opening into a high cavern. If there is not too much water issuing it may be possible to continue downstream; otherwise go back to the road and take a higher path through a flowery field, detouring to inspect the capricious course of the beck. Cross its dry bed near a barn to join Philpin Lane.

continued

HAWES 11¼

Weathercote House

school

Hill Inn

WINTER SCALES

Church

ROAD

SOUTHER SCALES

1100

1000

Chapel le Dale

THWAITE LANE

INGLETON

1: Weathercote Cave
2: Jingle Pot
3: Hurtle Pot

Ellerbeck

ford

NOTE:
New fencing in the vicinity and downstream of Gatekirk Cave suggests that visits to the cave are unwelcome. Enquire locally or at Broadrake.

Farm road

1000

Gill Head

farm road

1000

Philpin

ROAD (Philpin Lane)

1000

ROAD B6255

HAWES 11¼

Hill Inn

continued

Weathercote Cave

St. Leonard's Church,
Chapel-le-Dale

Whernside, from Bruntscar

A resurgence near Gatekirk Cave

Bruntscar Cave

New caves are still being discovered, but the obvious
entrances and potholes have been known since man first
settled in the district. The discovery of Bruntscar Cave,
however, is a remarkable story. The 17th-century house
at Bruntscar was built against a low limestone scar,
but it was not until 1865 that the then owner, curious
about the rumbling of underground water, broke a way
into the cliff behind the house and revealed a fine cave
that penetrates a third of a mile under Whernside. To
see it, apply at the adjoining house and offer a donation.

Gatekirk Cave

THE ASCENT OF INGLEBOROUGH

via GREAT DOUK CAVE
returning via MEREGILL HOLE

6 miles

from CHAPEL LE DALE (HILL INN)

THE OUTWARD JOURNEY:
A roadside gate 150 yards above the Hill Inn gives access to a good track (which may also be joined from a stile in the topiary hedge adjoining the inn) and this can be followed, although becoming indistinct, past Great Douk Cave to the wall beyond Middle Washfold. The climb alongside to 2000' is very tedious, but is succeeded by an exhilarating high-level traverse to the summit.

INGLEBOROUGH 2373'

Simon Fell

foot of the east ridge

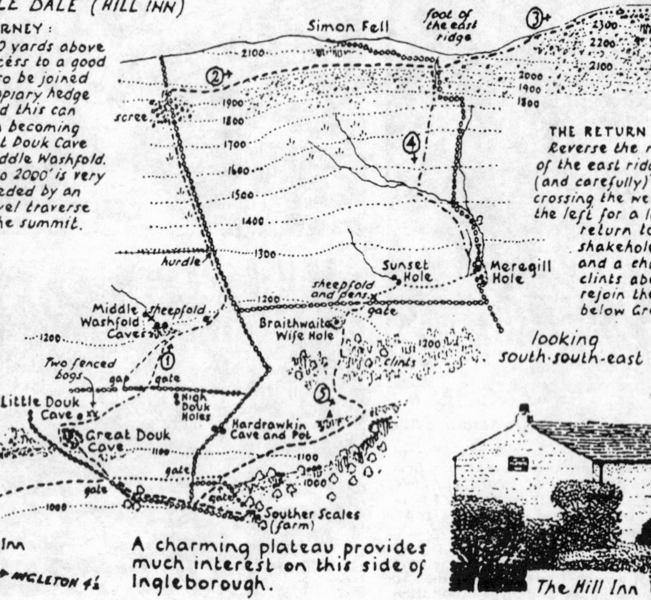

THE RETURN JOURNEY:
Reverse the route of ascent to the foot of the east ridge, where descend steeply (and carefully) by a broken wall to a path crossing the wet moor beyond. Incline to the left for a look at Meregill Hole, then return to the Hill Inn via the huge shakehole of Braithwaite Wife Hole and a charming path through the clints above Souther Scales Farm to rejoin the outward route at the gate below Great Douk Cave.

looking south-south-east

old limekiln

Middle Washfold Cave

Sunset Hole

Meregill Hole

sheepfold and dens

Braithwaite Wife Hole

Two fenced bogs

Little Douk Cave

High Douk Holes

gate

Great Douk Cave

Hardrawkin Cave and Pot

old limekiln

perched boulder

snow fence

gate

gate

gate

gate

Hill Inn

Souther Scales (farm)

Chapel le Dale

INGLETON 4½

A charming plateau provides much interest on this side of Ingleborough.

The Hill Inn

MAP

25
(2)

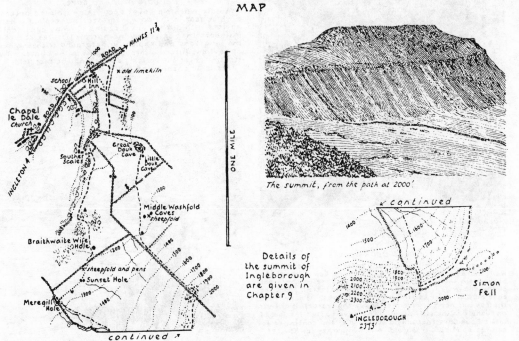

The summit, from the path at 2000'

Details of
the summit of
Ingleborough
are given in
Chapter 9

ONE MILE

continued →

← continued

ROAD TO HAWES 11¾

× old limekiln

school

Hill
Inn

Chapel
le Dale
Church

INGLETON 4

Southern
Scales

Great
Douk
Cave

Little
Douk
Cave

1200

Middle Washfold
Caves
× sheepfold

Braithwaite Wife
Hole

1200

1400

1500

1600

1700

sheepfold and pens

Sunset Hole

1300

1400

1800

1900

2000

Meregill
Hole

1400

1500

1600

1700

1800

1900

2000

2100

2200

2300

2100

2000

Simon
Fell

△
INGLEBOROUGH
2373

Middle Washfold Caves

Middle Washfold Caves occur in an isolated outcrop, a white scar in the dark moor near a sheepfold. Here, novices with girths not exceeding 40" may confidently insinuate themselves in the narrow fissures carved in the limestone and explore underground with the help of daylight filtering through cracks in the clints. Two streams enter the system, one behind the sheepfold. This is an enchanting place.

Great Douk Cave

A huge rift, sheltering many trees and enclosed by a wall, marks the position of Great Douk Cave. A steep path down the western slope gives access to the floor of the chasm. A stream issues in a waterfall from the cave mouth, soon to sink amongst stones. Entry into the cave is not easy: either brave the waterfall or enter an eyehole in the cliff above. The cave passes the foot of **Little Douk Cave** (actually a 60' pothole) and continues to emerge at Middle Washfold — not a journey for novices.

the wet entrance

Sunset Hole

the dry entrance

Limestone fissures, Middle Washfold

THE ALUM POT CAVE SYSTEM

This is a simple walk, little more
than a stroll, but very rewarding
in spectacle and interest.

NOTE : *A fee of sixpence per head
is payable at North Cote in
exchange for permission to
visit Alum Pot and the caves.
It should be paid willingly —
Alum Pot is cheap at the price.*

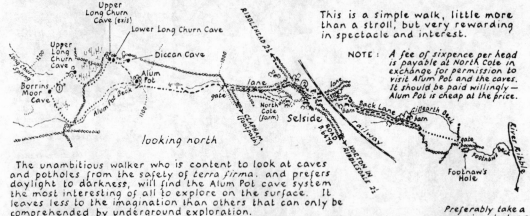

looking north

*Preferably take a
companion who has a
restraining influence
and some regard for
your life.*

 The unambitious walker who is content to look at caves
and potholes from the safety of terra firma, and prefers
daylight to darkness, will find the Alum Pot cave system
the most interesting of all to explore on the surface. It
leaves less to the imagination than others that can only be
comprehended by underground exploration.
 In particular, the overland tracking of the capricious Long Churn Spring
(the principal stream in the system) above its subterranean watercourse,
helped by its brief appearances above ground, is quite fascinating. For
short distances (indicated on page 3 of this chapter) the underground
channel may be followed with the aid of a torch.
 Although this walk, as described, is a pleasant relaxation and free from terrors, it is, however,
quite possible and in fact easy to die a horrible death by straying off-route. The dangers of
Alum Pot are manifestly obvious. Other deathtraps, unseen, occur in the black interiors of some
of the caves, Diccan Cave in particular being for expert adventurers only.

MAP

26
(2)

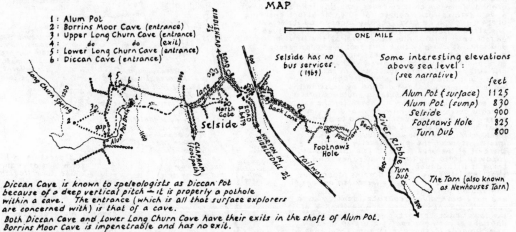

1 : Alum Pot
2 : Borrins Moor Cave (entrance)
3 : Upper Long Churn Cave (entrance)
4 :   do   do   (exit)
5 : Lower Long Churn Cave (entrance)
6 : Diccan Cave (entrance)

ONE MILE

Selside has no
bus services.
(1969)

Some interesting elevations
above sea level :
(see narrative)

	feet
Alum Pot (surface)	1125
Alum Pot (sump)	830
Selside	900
Footnaw's Hole	825
Turn Dub	800

Long Churn Spring

RIBBLEHEAD ROAD

Selside

North Cote

CLAPHAM
(footpath)

Alum Pot Beck

gap

HORTON IN RIBBLESDALE 2½

railway

Back Lane

Footnaw's Beck

Footnaw's
Hole

River Ribble

Turn Dub

The Tarn (also known
as Newhouses Tarn)

Diccan Cave is known to speleologists as Diccan Pot
because of a deep vertical pitch — it is properly a pothole
within a cave. The entrance (which is all that surface explorers
are concerned with) is that of a cave.
Both Diccan Cave and Lower Long Churn Cave have their exits in the shaft of Alum Pot.
Borrins Moor Cave is impenetrable and has no exit.

200 yards up the Ribblehead road from Selside hamlet, a rough lane branches off to the left (room to park a car
at the corner). Take this, and in 100 yards a stile in the wall may be used to call at North Cote farm to pay the
fee. Duty done, return to the lane and continue along it to a right-angled turn. Here use the facing gate or stile
and proceed along a former quarry track, which fades, to reach the plantation of trees ahead: here is Alum Pot,
which may be inspected from outside its enclosing wall, or, with care, an encircling path within the wall gives more
intimate views. Suitably impressed, return to the point where Alum Pot Beck plunges into the abyss. It is usual now to
visit the Long Churn caves next, but, in order to follow the system from its beginnings (the logical way), turn along
the course of Alum Pot Beck (upstream !!!), using the gap provided for it to cross a wall to do likewise. Beyond here is
rough moorland, with limestone interspersed. Make next for Borrins Moor Cave, which is not easy to find, and then
in turn visit Upper and Lower Long Churn and Diccan Caves before returning (overland !!!) to Alum Pot and Selside.
 The second part of the walk, from Selside to Footnaw's Hole and return, is recommended only with reservations:
Back Lane is surfaced with hundreds of individual cowclaps fused by rain into one major communal river of manure.

The feeders of Alum Pot

LONG CHURN SPRING rises high on the slopes of Park Fell and descends rough moorland to sink at 1250' into swampy ground, from which it emerges into daylight and follows a well-defined rocky course for 50 yards before entering UPPER LONG CHURN CAVE (readily located by its trees). The stream flows along the cave and can be pursued on foot until it falls into a deep pool at the limit of daylight. It is a pity that this pool is too dangerous an obstacle for the non-expert: were it not, the cave-passage could be followed without further difficulty for 250 yards to its exit in the next field. Discretion being much better than valour, make the journey above ground by crossing the wall at a point where abutting boulders form a convenient stile and aiming north for the exit, which is overhung by a hawthorn and adjoins a cross-wall. No stream emerges, and to discover what has happened to it enter the low passage for 20 yards, where it will be found vanishing into a fissure on the left. Directly opposite the exit of the upper cave, a few yards away, is LOWER LONG CHURN CAVE entrance, and there is little doubt that the two caves once formed a continuous passage and have been given separate identity by a roof fall. Go into the dry stony entrance of the lower cave; progress is facilitated by daylight entering a roof-fissure 10 yards in and 10 yards further the stream from the upper cave will be rejoined as it comes in on the right in a fine waterfall. If courage is high, it can be followed down, by wading, to a point where it abandons the cave in favour of a low passage on the left. Go no further. Return to the entrance and go down the field, passing the open roof-fissure, until, beyond a corner of the wall, the stream will be seen emerging and running overland for 12 yards before entering Diccan Cave, which conveys it underground into the depths of Alum Pot. Say goodbye to it and let it do the journey alone.

Borrins Moor Cave (described on page 5)

After surveying the area it will be clear that Long Churn Spring formerly flowed underground all the way from point A to Alum Pot, carving a continuous cave, which it has since abandoned in places for new channels, taking a short cut halfway and ending its career at a lower level in another cave, i.e. Diccan.

Underground passages shown on this map are approximate (intelligent conjecture)

A depression in the form of a dry valley running down from the southeast corner of Alum Pot suggests that in ages past, before the ground collapsed and gave the pot a surface opening, Alum Pot Beck may have flowed over it without interruption and continued down the hill to the Ribble.

ALUM POT BECK, the only surface feeder of Alum Pot, is normally of small volume but can be a torrent in wet weather; in times of drought its bed often dries up completely. It rises on Park Fell and pursues an erratic course on reaching the limestone strata, but has nothing of special interest.

100 yards

clints
roof fissure
Lower Long Churn Cave
Diccan Cave
Alum Pot
dry valley
Upper Long Churn Cave
boulders (cross wall here)
Alum Pot Beck
gap

KEY:
〜〜〜 surface stream   ‑‑‑‑‑ underground stream
∵∵∵∵ dry cave (no stream)   ≋≋≋ cave with stream

Alum Pot

Alum Pot, picturesquely embowered in trees and enclosed by a wall, is a spectacular and awe-inspiring vertical shaft, one of the best in the district. It has a long history of siege and conquest, the first descent being effected as long ago as 1847.

The stream entering the huge surface opening at the southwest corner, Alum Pot Beck, falls sheer to the depths in a 200' waterfall. It then descends in cascades a further 100 feet, almost, to a final pool at the bottom of the pot.

Unseen from the surface, far down in the gloom, a more considerable torrent, Long Churn Spring, also plunges into the pool from an opening (the exit of Diccan Cave) in the north wall of the shaft. Above this aperture, and dimly discernible from the surface, is another: the dry exit of the lower Long Churn Cave.

The pool, or sump, at the bottom of the pothole drains into an impenetrable, uncharted 'master cave' that may well pass underneath the hamlet of Selside. Its waters appear in daylight again at a sinister pool in Footnaw's Hole, a mile from Alum Pot and not far from the River Ribble, the difference in elevation being so slight that the passage of water from the bottom of Alum Pot to Footnaw's Hole takes several days. Strangely, after leaving Footnaw's Hole (underground again) the waters next appear, not in the River Ribble, for which they are obviously destined, but in a pond named Turn Dub on the far bank, having in fact passed underneath the river. From Turn Dub they flow overland, quite sedately, to the river, joining it as a tributary on the east side. (After a period of exceptionally heavy rain, Footnaw's Hole may fill to the brim, the surplus water then draining off along the normally dry course of the Footnaw's Beck and so joining the Ribble on the west side). This odd behaviour of the Alum Pot waters was first proved by chemical tests in 1901.

Alum Pot

Borrins Moor Cave

Borrins Moor Cave is not strictly a part
of the Long Churn system, being without
a stream. The cave is in a green hollow
of the moorland and is of unpromising
appearance, but, after scrambling over
a large boulder obstructing the entrance,
the cave passage will be found to be high
and roomy and easy to follow. 40 yards
in, on the right, a side passage, initially
awkward, gives good fast walking for 250
yards, the roof height being a uniform 6'.
For a novice cave explorer wishing to test
his nerves, this cave is one of the safest.

Upper Long Churn Cave (entrance)

PENYGHENT

Newhouses Tarn

Ribblesdale

Alum Pot

DICCAN CAVE

roof·fissure

Diccan Cave
(entrance)

Lower Long Churn Cave (entrance)
as seen from the exit of Upper Long Churn Cave

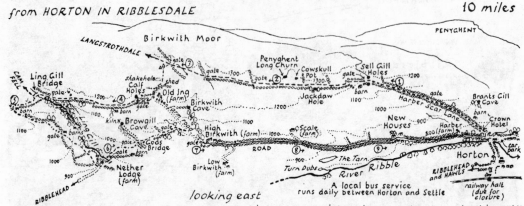

looking east

A local bus service
runs daily between Horton and Settle

The walk starts and finishes at the Crown Hotel and is best done anti-clockwise, reserving the roadwalking until the end of the day. On the outward route via Sell Gill the roughnesses of Harber Scar Lane are succeeded for 2 miles by an excellent green path (the old Settle-Langstrothdale packhorse road) before deviating across country to Old Ing — mark well the place of deviation: a low cairned hill on the left beyond a gate. At Old Ing another excellent path, at first muddy, leads to Ling Gill Bridge (this is the old Settle-Hawes packhorse road), skirting the brink of the deep wooded ravine of Ling Gill. Cross the bridge, here leaving the path and aiming west alongside a wall for a quarter of a mile to a barn, whence a path of sorts can be followed down to Nether Lodge. Cross the gill here by the bridge behind the farmhouse and pass through the facing gate to reach God's Bridge by an indistinct path, there making a detour upstream to visit Browgill Cave, where the stream emerges. Return to God's Bridge and continue south to join a farm road just above High Birkwith farm (once a wayside inn). Three unattractive miles on a tarmac road (where a lift should be accepted if offered) return the walker to the Crown Hotel.

North Ribblesdale is a wide expanse of rolling moors, with desolation the keynote — its beauties are hidden away in the wooded ravines that carry its streams down to the Ribble. The finest of these is Ling Gill, visited on this interesting expedition.

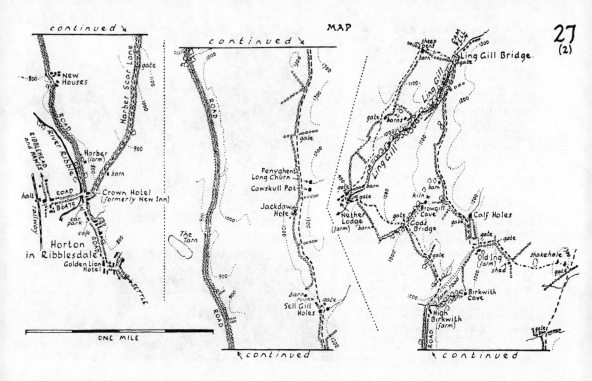

MAP

27
(2)

continued →

continued →

sheep pen

barn

Ling Gill Bridge.

1200

Ling Gill

1100

1200

1100

gate

New Houses

800

gate

1100

900

Harber Scar Lane

gate

barns

Ling Gill

1100

1200

ROAD

River Ribble

RIBBLEHEAD and MINES

Harber (farm)

800

900

barn

ROAD

1000

gate

barn

1200

gate

barn

kiln

Browgill Cove

Calf Holes

halt

ROAD

B6479

car park

café

Crown Hotel (formerly New Inn)

Penyghent Long Churn

Cowskull Pot

1100

gate

Nether Lodge (farm)

gate

barn

God's Bridge

gate

1000

gate

gate

Railway

ROAD

800

The Tarn

Jackdaw Hole

1200

1300

1000

1000

gate

Old Ing (farm) shed

shakehole

gate

Horton in Ribblesdale

900

Golden Lion Hotel

SETTLE

1000

1000

1000

Birkwith Cave

High Birkwith (farm)

ROAD

gate

barn ruins

gate

Sell Gill Holes

1300

1200

ONE MILE

← continued

← continued

← continued

Several interesting caves and potholes are passed on the walk and others may be inspected by short detours. In walking order they; are:

- **BRANTS GILL CAVE :** In a clump of trees across a field from a gate in Harber Scar Lane (no public footpath). Here emerges the stream that falls into Hunt Pot.

- **SELL GILL HOLES :** Stream entrance on the east side of the natural bridge crossed by the track; pothole entrance on the west. Opens into a huge underground cavern.

- **JACKDAW HOLE :** An open chasm amongst trees, surrounded by a wall.

- **COWSKULL POT :** A straight shaft, 70 feet deep, in a hollow of the moor east of track.

- **PENYGHENT LONG CHURN :** In an obvious stream bed 100 yards east of track. Stream falls into crevice 90 feet deep.

- **CALF HOLES :** At the end of the walled lane beyond Old Ing, on the right. Access by stile in wall. Stream sinks in rocky bed. Fenced.

- **GOD'S BRIDGE :** Brow Gill Beck flows into a short cave forming a natural bridge.

- **BROWGILL CAVE :** Follow Brow Gill Beck up the field to its debouchure from a fine cave. There is an underground passage (for experts only) to Calf Holes, where the stream sinks.

- **BIRKWITH CAVE :** At the head of the wooded gill above High Birkwith. Stream emerges.

Browgill Cave may be entered and penetrated in safety for 70 yards. All the others are dangerous to explore. Keep children and dogs on a tight leash.

Ling Gill

Ling Gill Bridge

God's Bridge

This old limekiln near Browgill Cave has
survived years of disuse remarkably well
and is one of the best-preserved in the
district. Note the fine chimney brickwork.

Browgill Cave

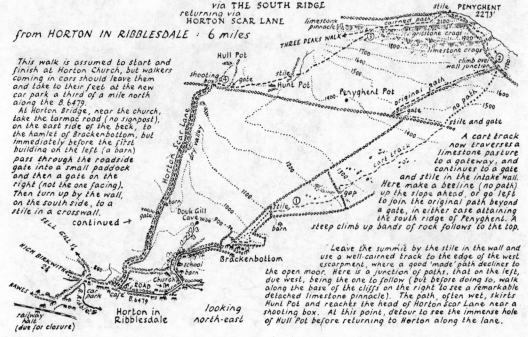

THE ASCENT OF PENYGHENT

via THE SOUTH RIDGE
returning via
HORTON SCAR LANE

from HORTON IN RIBBLESDALE : 6 miles

This walk is assumed to start and
finish at Horton Church, but walkers
coming in cars should leave them
and take to their feet at the new
car park a third of a mile north
along the B.6479.

At Horton Bridge, near the church,
take the tarmac road (no signpost),
on the east side of the beck, to
the hamlet of Brackenbottom, but
immediately before the first
building on the left (a barn)
pass through the roadside
gate into a small paddock
and then a gate on the
right (not the one facing).
Then turn up by the wall,
on the south side, to a
stile in a crosswall.

continued →

PENYGHENT 2273'

THREE PEAKS WALK

limestone pinnacle

cairned path

gritstone crags

limestone crags

climb over wall junction

Hull Pot

shooting box

gate

stile

Hunt Pot

Penyghent Pot

original path

no path

gate

stile and gate

A cart track
now traverses a
limestone pasture
to a gateway, and
continues to a gate
and stile in the intake wall.
Here make a beeline (no path)
up the slope ahead, or go left
to join the original path beyond
a gate, in either case attaining
the south ridge of Penyghent. A
steep climb up bands of rock follows to the top.

cart track

gap

stile

barn

Horton Scar Lane

dry valley

barn

gate

Douk Gill Cave

SELL GILL ↓↓

HIGH BIRKWITH 2¼

HAWES

railway halt
(due for closure)

school
barn

Church

ROAD

car park
café

B.6479

Horton in
Ribblesdale

*looking
north-east*

Brackenbottom

Leave the summit by the stile in the wall and
use a well-cairned track to the edge of the west
escarpment, where a good 'made' path declines to
the open moor. Here is a junction of paths, that on the left,
due west, being the one to follow (but before doing so, walk
along the base of the cliffs on the right to see a remarkable
detached limestone pinnacle). The path, often wet, skirts
Hunt Pot and reaches the head of Horton Scar Lane near a
shooting box. At this point, detour to see the immense hole
of Hull Pot before returning to Horton along the lane.

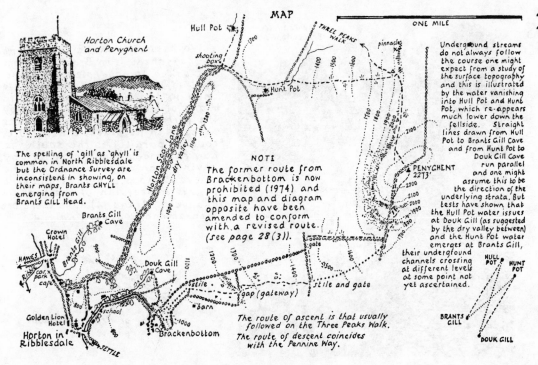

Horton Church and Penyghent

The spelling of 'gill' as 'ghyll' is common in North Ribblesdale but the Ordnance Survey are inconsistent in showing, on their maps, Brants GHYLL emerging from Brants GILL Head.

NOTE
The former route from Brackenbottom is now prohibited (1974) and this map and diagram opposite have been amended to conform with a revised route. (see page 28 (3)).

Underground streams do not always follow the course one might expect from a study of the surface topography and this is illustrated by the water vanishing into Hull Pot and Hunt Pot, which re-appears much lower down the fellside. Straight lines drawn from Hull Pot to Brants Gill Cave and from Hunt Pot to Douk Gill Cave run parallel and one might assume this to be the direction of the underlying strata. But tests have shown that the Hull Pot water issues at Douk Gill (as suggested by the dry valley between) and the Hunt Pot water emerges at Brants Gill, their underground channels crossing at different levels at some point not yet ascertained.

The route of ascent is that usually followed on the Three Peaks Walk.
The route of descent coincides with the Pennine Way.

PENYGHENT 2273'

Hull Pot   Hunt Pot
Brants Gill
Douk Gill

The road to
Brackenbottom

Walkers who make the ascent
of Penyghent from Brackenbottom
are asked to note, please, that a
part of the route, in common use
until 1974 although not a public
right of way, is now prohibited by
the farmer, who no longer permits
access. In its place, a new route,
roughly parallel to the south, is
now recommended, a right of way
having been established.   The
relevant maps, diagrams and text
in this impression of the book (i.e.
Chapters 28 and 34) have therefore
been amended accordingly.

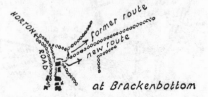

at Brackenbottom

Penyghent

The southern aspect

Penyghent (a name usually taken to mean 'Hill of the winds') has an impressive profile to the south, where the gritstone cap of the fell rests naked upon a band of limestone, both having weathered into steep crags. In this respect it is similar to Ingleborough and less obviously so to Whernside.

Penyghent is the lowest in altitude of the 'big three' but geographically it is the most important, its summit ridge dividing the west-flowing and east-flowing streams. Neither Ingleborough nor Whernside form part of the true watershed of northern England, both draining exclusively to the Irish Sea.

The summit is grassy, with a large cairn and an Ordnance column (5.577b) near a substantial wall that crosses the top from end to end. Rockclimbing is practiced on the surrounding ramparts.

The view is outstandingly good, covering much of the country of the Yorkshire Dales and north Lancashire to Morecambe Bay. The northern part of the Lakeland skyline is concealed but enough is in view to emphasise its supremacy over all other horizons.

Striated rocks, gritstone cliff, south ridge.

The summit

28
(4)

Hull Pot

Saxifraga oppositifolia

April visitors will ever afterwards remember Penyghent as the mountain of the purple saxifrage, for in April this beautiful plant decorates the white limestone cliffs on the 1900' contour with vivid splashes of colour, especially being rampant along the western cliff (overlooking the descent to Hunt Pot), which it drapes like aubretia on a garden wall.

Limestone pinnacle

The gritstone cap of Penyghent is succeeded by a dull moorland, on the descent to Horton, until surface limestone is reached at the contour of 1300'. Here is a 'classic' pothole area, and although several of the apertures are inconspicuous the two best known, Hull Pot and Hunt Pot — widely different in character — are readily located and may be visited with little loss of time. Hull Pot is an open chasm of remarkable size, 300' long, 60' wide and 60' deep; the waterfall, illustrated in the drawing, occurs only after heavy rainstorms, the stream normally sinking into its bed before reaching the pot. Hunt Pot is an evil slit, 15' long, 6' wide, and 200' deep, engulfing a stream. Both holes are enclosed by post and wire fencing and their dangers are obvious. The disappearing waters emerge from caves at Douk Gill Scar and Brants Gill Head near Horton.

Hunt Pot

STAINFORTH BRIDGE AND CATRIGG FORCE

from LANGCLIFFE

4½ miles

The Ribble's loveliest bridge and Craven's finest waterfall are featured in this beautiful walk.

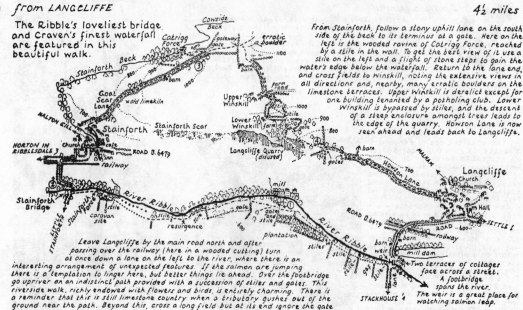

From Stainforth, follow a stony uphill lane on the south side of the beck to its terminus at a gate. Here on the left is the wooded ravine of Catrigg Force, reached by a stile in the wall. To get the best view of it use a stile on the left and a flight of stone steps to gain the water's edge below the waterfall. Return to the lane end and cross fields to Winskill, noting the extensive views in all directions and, nearby, many erratic boulders on the limestone terraces. Upper Winskill is derelict except for one building tenanted by a potholing club. Lower Winskill is bypassed by stiles, and the descent of a steep enclosure amongst trees leads to the edge of the quarry. Howson Lane is now seen ahead and leads back to Langcliffe.

looking east

Leave Langcliffe by the main road north and after passing over the railway (here in a wooded cutting) turn at once down a lane on the left to the river, where there is an interesting arrangement of unexpected features. If the salmon are jumping there is a temptation to linger here, but better things lie ahead. Over the footbridge go upriver on an indistinct path provided with a succession of stiles and gates. This riverside walk, richly endowed with flowers and birds, is entirely charming. There is a reminder that this is still limestone country when a tributary gushes out of the ground near the path. Beyond this, cross a long field but at its end ignore the gate into the caravan site and use a half-hidden stile to regain the river's edge and reach Stainforth Force with the bridge now in sight ahead.

MAP

29
(2)

Stainforth Bridge

The elegant arch of Stainforth Bridge has spanned the Ribble for three centuries, originally serving the packhorse traffic on an old highway linking Lancaster and York. New routes, modern roads and heavy vehicles have made the bridge redundant, but, as a possession of the National Trust, it remains as a graceful ornament of mellowed stone in perfect harmony with its sylvan surroundings, a reminder of days past when humble men had an eye for beauty and a pride in creating it, an enduring tribute to craftsmanship and good taste...... The bad old days, some folk call them.

Stainforth Force

At Stainforth Force the river rushes over limestone ledges into a black and sinister pool 30 feet deep, a fearsome place overhung by trees.
Force is an appropriately descriptive name, but there is not the single waterfall here usually associated with the name. In former days the place was known as Stainforth Foss.

ONE MILE

to HORTON 3
HALTON GILL
Church
Stainforth Beck
Stainforth Bridge
LITTLE STAINFORTH 4
Stainforth Force
Stainforth
Goal Scar Lane
Catrigg Force
Cowside Beck
800
caravan site
railway
1000
1100
River Ribble
Upper Winskill
Lower Winskill
old road
1000
900
600
Mill
800
STACKHOUSE 1
River Ribble
ROAD B 6479
railway
Howson Lane
800
MALHAM
mill road
railway
Church
Langcliffe
to SETTLE 1

Catrigg Force

Catrigg Force is a double waterfall of 60 feet in a very lovely setting.
Its older name, still used, is Catterick Foss.

The Big Tree

Langcliffe

Langcliffe, situated just off the main road and happily undisturbed by traffic, is a quiet village set around a pleasant green. Among its attractions are many picturesque cottages, a beautiful 17th century Hall, a 'big tree' and a fountain. On the wall of a building opposite the telephone kiosk is a tablet of 'The Naked Woman' (once an inn), evidence of sex being concealed by the date 1660. (3 years older than Settle's 'Naked Man').

Stainforth Force

Stainforth Bridge

*Stepping stones
at Stainforth*

Catrigg Force

looking north-east

·Jubilee Caves are also known as Foxholes.

Settle has an excellent museum (privately owned) of exceptional interest.

Leave Settle's Market Place by way of Constitution Hill, to the left of the Shambles, and when the road turns left take the rough lane (Banks Lane) branching uphill on the right. An iron gate above the wood opens into the field behind the limestone crag of Castlebergh, a remarkable vantage point with an exciting birds-eye view of the town below. Access to the flagpole on the top of the crag is barred by a wall, which, since most visitors will climb it, ought to have a built-in stile but hasn't. Then go back to Banks Lane and continue up it. (This detour to Castlebergh may be postponed and done on the return journey, if preferred).

Beyond the plantation at the top of Banks Lane a green path slants uphill to a gap in a wall and becomes more distinct as it enters a long dry valley aiming directly for Attermire below a succession of scars on the left: a strange and impressive scene. At the end of this valley Attermire Cave can be seen high in the cliffs ahead and may be visited by a steep scramble, needing care. The route now goes left, ascending into a higher valley with scars on the right containing several caves including the renowned Victoria Cave (not seen from the path but located at the top of an obvious scree slope with tracks leading up). A detour to the interesting Jubilee Caves can also be made before descending by cart-track to the Langcliffe-Malham road, returning thence to Banks Lane through pastures by an invisible path provided with gates, above the village of Langcliffe, charmingly seen.

A fine walk of exceptional interest and beauty, visiting some well-known caves in typical limestone scars.

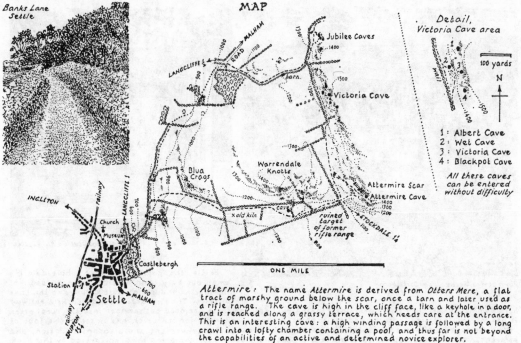

Banks Lane
Settle

MAP

Detail,
Victoria Cave area

Jubilee Caves
1400

MALHAM ROAD

LANGCLIFFE L.

barn

1500

Victoria Cave

100 yards

N

1: Albert Cave
2: Wet Cave
3: Victoria Cave
4: Blackpot Cave

*All these caves
can be entered
without difficulty*

INCLETON

railway

LANGCLIFFE L.

Blue
Crags

Warrendale
Knotts

1300

1200

Attermire Scar

Attermire Cave
1400
1300
1200

STOCKDALE 1½

Church
Museum

x old kiln

cave

ruined
target of
former rifle range

Castlebergh

Station

Settle

MALHAM

railway

ONE MILE

Attermire: The name *Attermire* is derived from *Otters Mere*, a flat
tract of marshy ground below the scar, once a tarn and later used as
a rifle range. The cave is high in the cliff face, like a keyhole in a door,
and is reached along a grassy terrace, which needs care at the entrance.
This is an interesting cave: a high winding passage is followed by a long
crawl into a lofty chamber containing a pool, and thus far is not beyond
the capabilities of an active and determined novice explorer.

Town centre, Settle, from Castleberah

A corner of Constitution Hill, Settle

Settle

Settle, the 'capital' of Upper Ribblesdale, is a small but busy town astride the main road A65 linking the industrial West Riding and the Lake District. The still-active Leeds-Carlisle railway here commences its long climb over the Pennine outliers and there are good bus services into the rural areas. It has many interesting features and picturesque corners, unchanged for centuries, and is set at the foot of lofty limestone hills that contribute much to its attractiveness. Its convenient and pleasant situation, and awareness of the needs of visitors, make it an excellent centre for exploring the area covered by this book.

Warrendale Knotts

Limestone escarpments (locally *scars*) usually take the form of long cliffs fissured horizontally in layers or bedding planes and vertically in cracks and gullies, often revealing the effect of pressures quite noticeably. Warrendale Knotts do not conform to this pattern, having the shape of isolated tors greatly eroded and shattered, like crumbling fortresses, the tops having a serrated outline that makes the group very distinctive and readily identifiable from long distances.

In the illustration on the left, the black patch is NOT a blot (perish the thought!) but the entrance to a small cave so snug and dry a refuge in wet weather that one regrets going past on a fine day. It is near the path and in full view.

Attermire Scar

*The position of
Attermire Cave
is indicated
by arrows*

VICTORIA CAVE

STOCKDALE

SETTLE

path to Attermire Cave

Victoria Cave

The imposing entrance to Victoria Cave is artificial, the result of man's efforts to gain easier access to the large cavern discovered by the curiosity of a dog and his master in 1837 — the year of Queen Victoria's coronation, hence the name — the original place of entry (still to be seen, high on the left) being an opening recessed in the rocks. First explorations were so rewarding that the present entrance was made and extensive excavations undertaken, yielding a fascinating and informative record of the occupation of the cave by man and beast through the ages ..... The topmost 'finds,' on or near the surface of the floor of the cave, were relics of early British occupation in and about the time of the Romans, below which a deposit of natural debris and clay indicated that the cave was untenanted for a lengthy period, but, six feet down, many evidences were found of occupation by Neolithic man and animals. Still deeper, beneath another deposit of earth, was found a bed containing remains of reindeer and bears including complete skulls of two grizzly bears. This was succeeded by a thick layer of glacial clay formed during the Ice Age, and this, when removed, exposed yet another level producing bones of many large animals, identified as bear, deer, rhinoceros, hippopotamus and ox. Thus, in layers superimposed one above another and separated by debris accumulated in periods of non-occupation was revealed the story of the former residents of Victoria Cave. No other cave has told its story so well or so graphically illustrated it by visual evidence, a collection of relics from the cave being on display in the museum at Settle.

Attermire Cave
(looking out)

Victoria Cave

Wet Cave

Jubilee Caves

THE ASCENT OF RYE LOAF HILL

via ATTERMIRE and STOCKDALE
returning via SCALEBER FORCE

7 miles

A splendid walk, full of interest, in contrasting scenery.

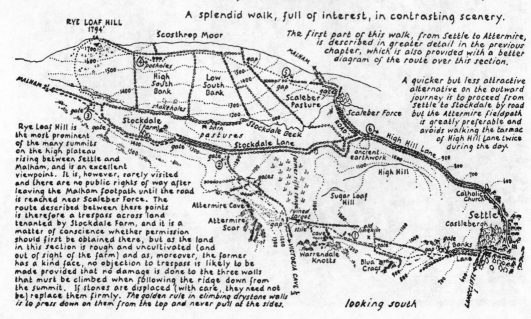

The first part of this walk, from Settle to Attermire, is described in greater detail in the previous chapter, which is also provided with a better diagram of the route over this section.

A quicker but less attractive alternative on the outward journey is to proceed from Settle to Stockdale by road but the Attermire fieldpath is greatly preferable and avoids walking the tarmac of High Hill Lane twice during the day.

Rye Loaf Hill is the most prominent of the many summits on the high plateau rising between Settle and Malham, and is an excellent viewpoint. It is, however, rarely visited and there are no public rights of way after leaving the Malham footpath until the road is reached near Scaleber Force. The route described between these points is therefore a trespass across land tenanted by Stockdale Farm, and it is a matter of conscience whether permission should first be obtained there, but as the land in this section is rough and uncultivated (and out of sight of the farm) and as, moreover, the farmer has a kind face, no objection to trespass is likely to be made provided that no damage is done to the three walls that must be climbed when following the ridge down from the summit. If stones are displaced (with care, they need not be) replace them firmly. *The golden rule in climbing drystone walls is to press down on them from the top and never pull at the sides.*

looking south

MAP

31
(2)

Stockdale lies along the line of the Craven Fault, and the contrast in terrain is very marked.   North of the beck is a charming green and white landscape typical of limestone, south is dark shaggy moorland characteristic of gritstone, peat-covered but appearing in outcrops on Rye Loaf Hill.   An intrusion of limestone occurs, however, on the south bank, being indicated by a few large shakeholes like bomb craters, but of no great significance.

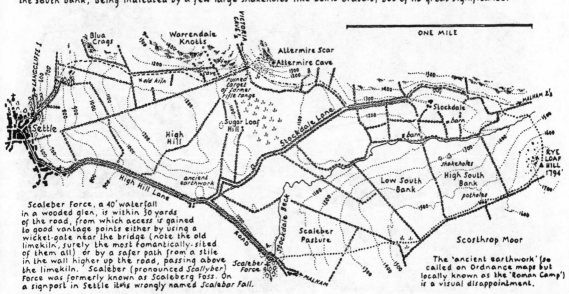

Scaleber Force, a 40' waterfall in a wooded glen, is within 30 yards of the road, from which access is gained to good vantage points either by using a wicket-gate near the bridge (note the old limekiln, surely the most romantically-sited of them all) or by a safer path from a stile in the wall higher up the road, passing above the limekiln.   Scaleber (pronounced Scallyber) Force was formerly known as Scaleberg Foss. On a signpost in Settle it is wrongly named Scalebar Fall.

The 'ancient earthwork' (so called on Ordnance maps but locally known as the 'Roman Camp') is a visual disappointment.

The summit of Rye Loaf Hill

Stockdale Farm and Rye Loaf Hill

Shakeholes, High South Bank

Scaleber Force

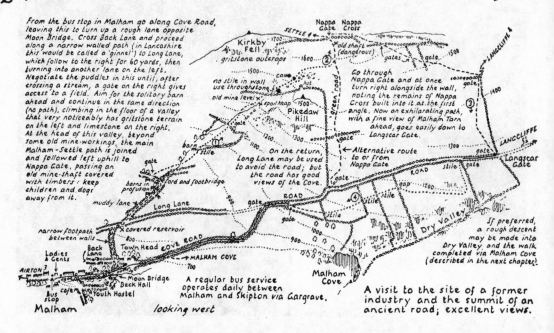

From the bus stop in Malham go along Cove Road, leaving this to turn up a rough lane opposite Moon Bridge. Cross Back Lane and proceed along a narrow walled path (in Lancashire this would be called a 'ginnel') to Long Lane, which follow to the right for 60 yards, then turning into another lane on the left. Negotiate the puddles in this until, after crossing a stream, a gate on the right gives access to a field. Aim for the solitary barn ahead and continue in the same direction (no path), climbing in the floor of a valley that very noticeably has gritstone terrain on the left and limestone on the right. At the head of this valley, beyond some old mine-workings, the main Malham–Settle path is joined and followed left uphill to Nappa Gate, passing an old mine-shaft covered with timbers: keep children and dogs away from it.

Go through Nappa Gate and at once turn right alongside the wall, noting the remains of Nappa Cross built into it at the first angle. Now an exhilarating path, with a fine view of Malham Tarn ahead, goes easily down to Langscar Gate.

On the return, Long Lane may be used to avoid the road; but the road has good views of the Cove.

← Alternative route to or from Nappa Gate

If preferred, a rough descent may be made into Dry Valley and the walk completed via Malham Cove (described in the next chapter).

A regular bus service operates daily between Malham and Skipton via Gargrave.

looking west

A visit to the site of a former industry and the summit of an ancient road; excellent views.

Map labels:
SETTLE
Nappa Gate
Nappa Cross
Kirkby Fell
gritstone outcrops
1700
1600
1500
LANGCLIFFE
old shaft (dangerous)
gates
gate
no stile in wall use throughstone
cove
Hut
old mine level
spoil heap
Pikedaw Hill
Green road
gate
1400
LANGCLIFFE
1300
Langscar Gate
gate
stile
gate
LANGSCAR ROAD
barn
stile
barns in profusion
ford and footbridge
gate
muddy lane
Long Lane
gate
ROAD
gap
1200
stile
stile
Dry Valley
narrow footpath between walls
X covered reservoir
Back Lane
Town Head
COVE ROAD
Ladies & Gents
AIRTON
Moon Bridge
Beck Hall
Bus stop
café
Youth Hostel
Malham
MALHAM COVE
700
800
900
1000
Malham Cove

MAP

32
(2)

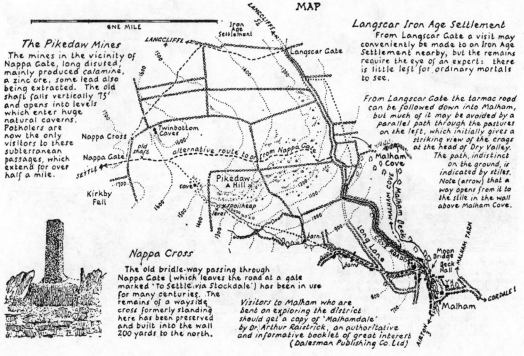

The Pikedaw Mines

The mines in the vicinity of Nappa Gate, long disused, mainly produced calamine, a zinc ore, some lead also being extracted. The old shaft falls vertically 75' and opens into levels which enter huge natural caverns. Potholers are now the only visitors to these subterranean passages, which extend for over half a mile.

Nappa Cross

The old bridle-way passing through Nappa Gate (which leaves the road at a gate marked 'To Settle via Stockdale') has been in use for many centuries. The remains of a wayside cross formerly standing here has been preserved and built into the wall 200 yards to the north.

Langscar Iron Age Settlement

From Langscar Gate a visit may conveniently be made to an Iron Age Settlement nearby, but the remains require the eye of an expert: there is little left for ordinary mortals to see.

From Langscar Gate the tarmac road can be followed down into Malham, but much of it may be avoided by a parallel path through the pastures on the left, which initially gives a striking view of the crags at the head of Dry Valley.

The path, indistinct on the ground, is indicated by stiles. Note (arrow) that a way opens from it to the stile in the wall above Malham Cove.

Visitors to Malham who are bent on exploring the district should get a copy of 'Malhamdale' by Dr. Arthur Raistrick, an authoritative and informative booklet of great interest (Dalesman Publishing Co. Ltd)

At Pikedaw: A disused mine level (keystone inscribed 1872) in the gritstone and a walled cave in the limestone.

Monk Bridge, Malham
Originally, a narrow packhorse bridge, later widened to accommodate vehicles. The width of the old bridge, some 3 feet, is clearly discernible under the arch.

Moon Bridge, Malham
Upstream of Beck Hall, this ancient clapper bridge of limestone slabs is named after its builder, Prior Moon.

The old shaft of the Pikedaw mine near Nappa Gate

The head of Dry Valley

GORDALE SCAR, MALHAM TARN AND MALHAM COVE
from MALHAM : 8 miles

Limestone scenery at its very best and most impressive.
A superb walk in unique surroundings.

NOTE FOR THE FAINT-HEARTED BEFORE STARTING:
The walk, as described, meets an impasse at
Gordale Scar that can only be overcome by
a short rock-climb.

Highfolds Scar

*Great
Close
Scar*

*Malham Tarn
House*

Malham Tarn

④

SETTLE 6

*Water
Sinks*

gate

*Dean Moor
Hill*

⑤

*Comb
Hill*

1200

PENNINE WAY

ROAD

③

NWHARFEDALE

*Prior
Rakes*

*cattle
grid*

stile

tumulus

*Seaty
Hill*

LANGCLIFFE 6
SETTLE 6¾

ROAD

*limestone
pavement*

DRY valley

1200

Broad Scars

1300

1100

Ⓒ

stile

PENNINE WAY

1200

*Malham
Cove*

Broad Flats

1200

1100

1100

Malham Beck

800

900

1000

*New Close
Knots*

900

② *Gordale beck*

stile

1000

1200

1100

1000

*Gordale
Scar*

900

800

Leave Malham by the road
going east to Gordale,
preferably detouring
to see Janet's Foss by
the route shown. Beyond
the road-bridge, on the left
a much-trodden field-entrance
is used. Proceed among beds of
watercress to the cliffs ahead.
Gordale Scar comes impressively
into view around a rocky corner.
The only way forward at the lower
waterfall is by a rockclimb of 20ft.
up the steep buttress on the left —
ample footholds make it easier than
it looks. A long slope of scree coming
down on the left is now ascended, passing
the upper waterfall (seen pouring through
a 'window' in the rocks). On easier ground
above, a fair path, initially indistinct, is
followed along the edge of the ravine, emerging
on the Malham Tarn road: turn right along it
to the tarn and Malham Tarn House. So endeth
the outward journey.

*Town
Head*

fall

700

ROAD (to Malham Tarn)

Cawden

900

gates

*Ladies and
Gents*

*Malham
bus stop*

café

stiles

ROAD

*old and new
bridges*

*barn
(ruin)*

barn

barn

*Gordale
House*

BORDLEY

Gordale Beck

cave

*Wedber
Brow*

barn

gates

Janet's Foss

800

*looking
northwest*

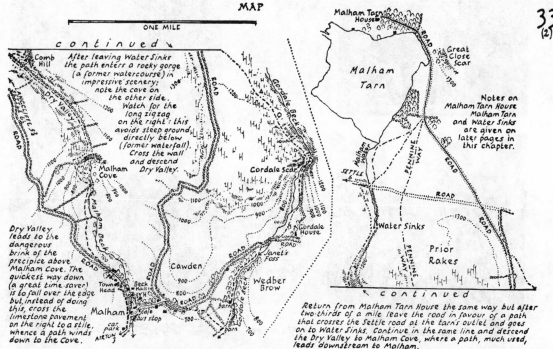

MAP

33
(2)

ONE MILE

c o n t i n u e d

Comb Hill

After leaving Water Sinks the path enters a rocky gorge (a former watercourse) in impressive scenery: note the cave on the other side.
Watch for the long zigzag on the right: this avoids steep ground directly below (former waterfall).
Cross the wall and descend Dry Valley.

DRY VALLEY

LANGCLIFFE ROAD

ROAD

Malham Cove

Cordale Scar

Gordale Beck

Malham Tarn House

Great Close Scar

Malham Tarn

Notes on Malham Tarn House Malham Tarn and Water Sinks are given on later pages in this chapter.

Dry Valley leads to the dangerous brink of the precipice above Malham Cove. The quickest way down (a great time-saver) is to fall over the edge but, instead of doing this, cross the limestone pavement on the right to a stile, whence a path winds down to the Cove.

Malham Beck

ROAD

Town Head

Beck Hall

Cawden

Cordale House

Janet's Fass

Wedber Brow

ROAD

barn

barn

Malham

cafe

bus stop

car park

AIRTON

Malham Water

SETTLE

PENNINE WAY

ROAD

Water Sinks

ROAD

Prior Rakes

PENNINE WAY

c o n t i n u e d

Return from Malham Tarn House the same way but after two-thirds of a mile leave the road in favour of a path that crosses the Settle road at the tarn's outlet and goes on to Water Sinks. Continue in the same line and descend the Dry Valley to Malham Cove, where a path, much used, leads downstream to Malham.

Janet's
Foss

Gordale
Scar

left:
    the waterfalls

The climb up the
buttress is shown
by a dotted line.
(The buttress is
    composed of
    a deposit of
    carbonate
    of lime
    known as
    tufa.)

right : the gorge

Malham Tarn House

One's first reaction on seeing Malham Tarn House is of wonderment
that such a splendid mansion should ever have been built here, in this
particular location, miles from anywhere and in the middle of a bleak
tableland 1350' above sea level. The site was originally occupied by a
shooting lodge, which seems more appropriate to the surroundings, the
present house being built over a century ago as a private residence: as
such it enjoyed visits from many literary celebrities. Charles Kingsley's
'Water Babies' was inspired by the scenery. Shorn of some of its original
ornate features, in particular a tower in the east wing, the property with
its extensive grounds is now owned by the National Trust and used as a
centre by the Council for Promotion of Field Studies. The natural life of
the area is preserved and protected, the resident staff catering for groups
of students and other interested visitors. Formerly the environs of Malham
Tarn were unfrequented and almost unknown outside the locality, but now,
on any summer weekend, the place attracts many people in sympathy with
the Council's objects and there is much pedestrian activity in the woods, on
the paths and by the shore, cars happily being prohibited from the reserve.
Once a shooting lodge for the destruction of birds, now a sanctuary for their
preservation. A gleam of hope for the human race, too!

Gordale Scar: looking down from the top of the scree run

Malham Tarn

Great Close Scar

Malham Tarn is a surprise. All around are the gleaming white cliffs and outcrops of limestone, and limestone, being porous, does not hold surface water, hence the labyrinth of subterranean passages, caves and potholes honeycombing the underworld of limestone country. Yet Malham Tarn is not only permanent but extensive, measuring roughly half-a-mile square. The explanation is geological, that it lies on a bed of harder rock, Silurian slate, which is impervious to water and recurs in patches along the line of the disturbance, the North Craven Fault, that influences the landscape hereabouts. The tarn is a sanctuary for birds and waterfowl, which enjoy here a life free from persecution.

Water Sinks

The stream issuing from Malham Tarn flows beneath the road south of the outlet and into the opposite field, where, after 300 yards, it silently vanishes underground in a bed of stones alongside a wall. This place is Water Sinks and from here, southwards, a dry grassy hollow suggests that at one time the stream continued an overland course along it, this appearing to be confirmed when an impressive ravine opens ahead between craggy heights and ends abruptly in a sharp drop with indications of a former waterfall. Below this, the valley turns southeast, still well-defined, still dry, to the brink of the great precipice falling sheer 240 feet to Malham Cove. A stream emerges from the base of the cliff, and it seems a safe bet that this is the stream last seen at Water Sinks, having made a subterranean journey underneath the valley it once occupied. But in limestone country the obvious cannot always be taken for granted, and in fact the stream from Water Sinks runs still further underground to reappear in daylight at Aire Head Springs, south of Malham village. (The stream emerging at the Cove has been proved by tests to originate beyond Langscar, northwest, sinking near the site of an old smelt mill).

There is no doubt, however, that the Dry Valley was carved by a retreating glacier and torrents of melt-water at the end of the Ice Age, and at that time a tremendous waterfall, higher than Niagara, must have poured into Malham Cove. Later, as the ice thawed in the limestone bed and admitted water into its fissures, a new course underground was adopted by the stream, leaving the Dry Valley and Malham Cove as they appear today — a strange and wonderful sculpturing by natural forces, yet out-moded by the passage of time.

Limestone pavement
above Malham Cove

Malham Cove

THE THREE PEAKS WALK

24 miles

The Three Peaks are our old friends, Whernside Ingleborough and Penyghent, which, being flat-topped, are strictly not peaks at all. This collective name for them is too flattering, but there is a fine challenge about it that inspires many walkers to attempt to reach all three summits and make a complete pedestrian circuit in a single one-day expedition. The Three Peaks Walk has become a recognised test of ability and endurance, and in recent years it has attracted increasing attention. Inevitably, and regrettably, it has become the subject of competitive races, both on foot and on wheel, and the breaking of records. With these attempts to accomplish the circuit in double-quick time, stop-watch in hand, we are not concerned here. The intention of this chapter is to detail the walk for the benefit of those whose main object in walking is pleasure and who climb hills for their intrinsic merit, for those who are not too preoccupied with tight timetables to study the landscape as they go along or turn aside to admire a shy saxifrage. Nevertheless, this is an undertaking for strong walkers only; not merely good walkers, but good walkers with staying power. It is a gruelling test of stamina. Many more walkers start the course than finish it. Many fall by the wayside, and some on stony ground.

Happily, it is a walk with few rules. The aim is to link the three summits on foot in a single walk, ending it at the place of starting, which may be any point on the route. Horton in Ribblesdale is most in favour, and the walk is here described as starting from and finishing at Horton Church, in an anti-clockwise direction (as suggested in the leaflet of the Youth Hostels Association, *The Three Peaks Walk*, price 6ᵈ). The detailed maps in this chapter are, however, serviceable whichever starting point is chosen and whichever direction is taken. But there is no set route, each walker being free to plan his own course, in doing which he should respect the laws of trespass and the country code.

Preferably, the walk should be attempted only with foreknowledge of the terrain, acquired on previous outings, and in clear and settled weather. The hours of daylight are too short in winter (never walk on limestone in the dark). 24 miles over rough hills, with nearly 5,000 feet of ascent and, of course, as much descent, is no Sunday School picnic. It is far too arduous a journey for walkers whose performances can only be described as 'fair to middling', but even such tortoises can earn a diluted fame by doing the walk a section at a time over a season, leisurely, and the odds are that they will enjoy the Three Peaks much more than the hares.

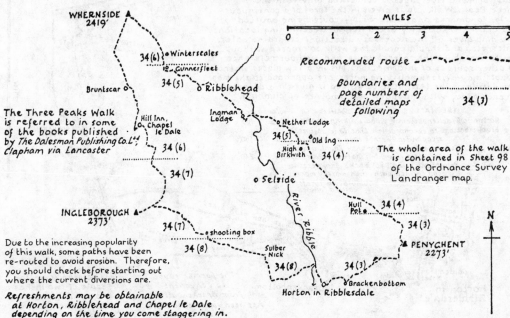

THE THREE PEAKS WALK
RECOMMENDED ROUTE

WHERNSIDE
2419'

MILES

0 1 2 3 4 5

34 (6) o Winterscales
        Gunnerfleet
34 (5) o Ribblehead

Recommended route ------

Boundaries and
page numbers of
detailed maps
following

34 (3)

Bruntscar o

Ingman
Lodge

The Three Peaks Walk
is referred to in some
of the books published
by *The Dalesman Publishing Co.L*;
Clapham via Lancaster

Hill Inn,
o Chapel
le Dale

34 (6)

34 (7)

o Nether Lodge

34 (5)
High o   o Old Ing
Birkwith
        34 (4)

The whole area of the walk
is contained in Sheet 98
of the Ordnance Survey
Landranger map.

o Selside

INGLEBOROUGH
2373'

34 (7)   o shooting box

34 (8)

Due to the increasing popularity
of this walk, some paths have been
re-routed to avoid erosion. Therefore,
you should check before starting out
where the current diversions are.

*Refreshments may be obtainable
at Horton, Ribblehead and Chapel le Dale
depending on the time you come staggering in.*

Hull
Pot o   34 (4)

34 (3)

River Ribble

Sulber
Nick

34 (8)

34 (3)

o
Horton in Ribblesdale

o Brackenbottom

PENYCHENT
2273'

N

continuation 34 (4)

The map starting on this page and continuing on the next following five pages is concerned only with the Three Peaks Walk. It is given in the form of a continuous strip, landmarks and features off-route being omitted to aid clarity, unless they are a help in determining location. The map gives all the necessary directions regarding gates, stiles, etc., and should enable the walk to proceed without hesitation about the correct route and without reference to other sources of information, but in a few places where doubts may arise amplifying notes are appended to the map. The nature of the terrain to be walked is given in side-notes on each page, with mileages and amounts of climbing.

THE NATURE OF THE TERRAIN :

	miles	ascent
Horton to Brackenbottom : Road walking (tarmac)	½	100'
Brackenbottom to second stile : Limestone pastures, steep initially, then easy gradient	1	560'
Second stile to Penyghent : Rough grass, then steep ridge to final easy grass slope	1	840'
Penyghent to Hull Pot Beck : Easy descent; good cairned path, then marshy moor	1½	—
Cumulative totals carried forward	4	1500'

HORTON
via Horton Scar Lane

PENYGHENT
2273'

climb wall
at junction

Douk Gill
Cave

former route now prohibited

stile

gateway

stile

RIBBLEHEAD and HAWES

Crown Hotel!

halt
railway

ROAD

Car ×
park
café

Golden Lion
Hotel

Horton in
Ribblesdale

school

barn

ROAD

SETTLE

Brackenbottom

The former route
to Penyghent
from Brackenbottom
has been superseded (1974).
See Chapter 28.

ONE MILE

The map is on the
scale of two inches
to a mile, and the
top of each page is
north.

MAP

34
(4)

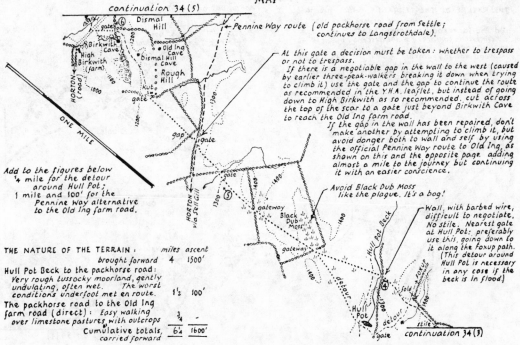

Continuation 34 (5)

Dismal
Hill

Pennine Way route (old packhorse road from Settle;
continues to Langstrothdale).

Birkwith
Cave

High
Birkwith
(farm)

Old Ing
Cave

Dismal Hill
Cave

Rough
Hill

HORTON (road)

1000

Hut

gate

1200

1300

gap

gate

At this gate a decision must be taken: whether to trespass
or not to trespass.
  If there is a negotiable gap in the wall to the west (caused
by earlier three-peak-walkers breaking it down when trying
to climb it) use the gate and the gap to continue the route
as recommended in the Y.H.A. leaflet, but instead of going
down to High Birkwith as so recommended, cut across
the top of the scar to a gate just beyond Birkwith Cave
to reach the Old Ing farm road.
  If the gap in the wall has been repaired, don't
make another by attempting to climb it, but
avoid danger both to wall and self by using
the official Pennine Way route to Old Ing, as
shown on this and the opposite page, adding
almost a mile to the journey but continuing
it with an easier conscience.

ONE MILE

Add to the figures below
  ¼ mile for the detour
    around Hull Pot;
  1 mile and 100' for the
    Pennine Way alternative
    to the Old Ing farm road.

HORTON via Sell Gill

1300

1400

1400

1500

gate

gateway

Black
Dub
Moss

Avoid Black Dub Moss
like the plague. It's a bog!

Hull Pot Beck

1400

Wall, with barbed wire,
difficult to negotiate.
No stile. Nearest gate
at Hull Pot; preferably
use this, going down to
it along the Foxup path.
(This detour around
Hull Pot is necessary
in any case if the
beck is in flood).

gateway

1400

1300

detour

FOXUP

fold

stile

detour

Hull
Pot

gate

continuation 34 (3)

THE NATURE OF THE TERRAIN :

	miles	ascent
brought forward	4	1500'
Hull Pot Beck to the packhorse road: Very rough tussocky moorland, gently undulating, often wet. The worst conditions underfoot met en route.	1½	100'
The packhorse road to the Old Ing farm road (direct): Easy walking over limestone pastures, with outcrops	¾	–
Cumulative totals, carried forward	6¼	1600'

MAP

THE NATURE OF THE TERRAIN: miles ascent
brought forward 6¼ 1600'
Old Ing farm road to Nether Lodge:
Limestone pastures; slight descent 1 20'
Nether Lodge to Ingman Lodge gate:
Road walking (gravel) 1¼ 90'
Ingman Lodge gate to Ribblehead:
Road walking (tarmac; B 6479) 1¼ 50'
Ribblehead to Gunnerfleet:
Level cart-track ¾ -

Cumulative totals 10½ 1760'
carried forward

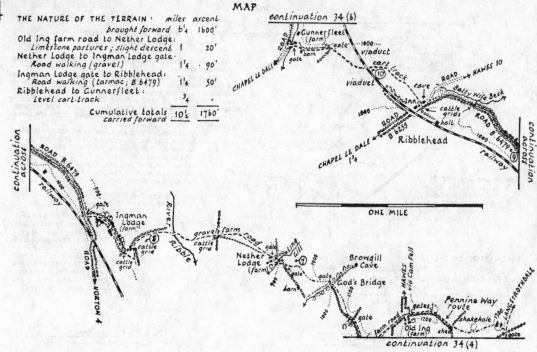

continuation 34 (b)

Gunnerfleet (farm)
CHAPEL LE DALE
gate
barn
viaduct
cart track
ROAD → HAWES 10
cave
Batty Wife Beck
inn
viaduct
cattle grids
halt
ROAD B 6255
Ribblehead
CHAPEL LE DALE 1¼
railway
continuation across

ONE MILE

continuation across
ROAD B 6479
railway
gate
Ingman Lodge (farm)
cattle grid
cattle grid
ROAD
HORTON 4
River Ribble
gravel farm road
cattle grid
gate
Nether Lodge (farm)
barn
Ling Gill
gate
gate
Browgill Cave
God's Bridge
HAWES via Cam Fell
gate
gates
shakehole
Pennine Way route
LANGSTROTHDALE
farm road
Old Ing (farm)
shed
gate

continuation 34 (4)

continuation
across ↑

cattle grids

WHERNSIDE
2419'

spring

This steady and unremitting climb up
Whernside is the most tedious and
tiring section of the walk; it is,
above 1200', the longest mile of all.
There is nothing exciting to see
and the treadmill becomes very
monotonous. The final few
hundred feet, although much
rougher and steeper, at least
hold a promise that the top
is near. The stream is a
good guide in mist.

High Pike

Low Pike

use throughstones
in wall as stile

INGLETON

At Winterscales
use the route
signposted by
the farmer

stile

ruin

gates

Winterscales
(farm)

gate

gate

barn

railway

IVESCAR ROAD

continuation 34(5)

cattle
grid

ROAD

900'

Philpin
(farm)

ROAD RIBBLEHEAD 1¾

cattle
grids

gate

x old limekiln

Hill
Inn

school

gate

Chapel
le Dale

INGLETON 4½

gate

Great Douk
Cave

Little Douk
Cave

two
fenced
bogs

gate

1200'

Middle
Washfold
Caves

sheepfold

continuation 34(7)

gate

barn

Broadrake
(farm)

gate barn

Bruntscar
(farm)

continuation
across ↑

THE NATURE OF THE TERRAIN:	miles	ascent
brought forward	10½	1760'
Gunnerfleet to Winterscales: Road walking (tarmac)	½	30'
Winterscales to Whernside: Rough moorland beyond the intakes, with a final very steep scree slope	1½	1400'
Whernside to the Hill Inn: Easy walk along grassy ridge, then down moor. Road (tarmac) from Bruntscar 2¾		70'
Hill Inn to Middle Washfold Caves Limestone pastures with outcrops	1	230'
Cumulative totals carried forward	16¼	3490'

MAP

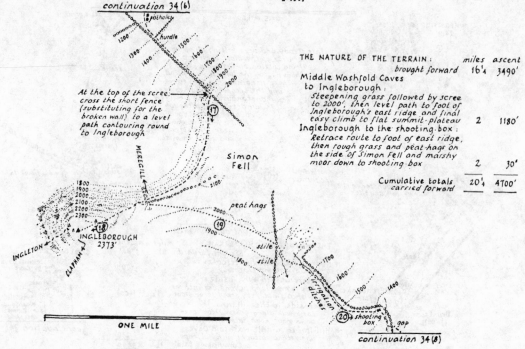

continuation 34(6)

potholes

1200
1300
1400
1500
1600
1700
1800
1900
2000

hurdle

At the top of the scree
cross the short fence
(substituting for the
broken wall) to a level
path contouring round
to Ingleborough

⑰

MERE GILL

Simon
Fell

1800
1900
2000
2100
2200
2300

peat hags

2100

2000

⑲

1900

1800

stile

stile

△ INGLEBOROUGH
2373

INGLETON

CLAPHAM

1700

1600

1500

1400

irrigation ditches

⑳ shooting box

gap

ONE MILE

THE NATURE OF THE TERRAIN :

	miles	ascent
brought forward	16¼	3490'

Middle Washfold Caves
to Ingleborough :

*Steepening grass followed by scree
to 2000', then level path to foot of
Ingleborough's east ridge and final
easy climb to flat summit-plateau*   2   1180'

Ingleborough to the shooting-box :

*Retrace route to foot of east ridge,
then rough grass and peat-hags on
the side of Simon Fell and marshy
moor down to shooting-box*   2   30'

Cumulative totals
carried forward   20¼   4700'

continuation 34(8)

MAP

34
(8)

continuation 34(7)

Sulber Pot

Nick Pot

gap

pool

SELSIDE

21

pool

pool

Sulber Nick

CLAPHAM

1200

The direct route from Sulber Nick to Beecroft Hall, although recommended in the Y.H.A. leaflet, is strictly a trespass, and a source of trouble to the farmer. (The leaflet is to be revised). The only right of way descending into Horton hereabouts is the public footpath from Crummack Dale. This should be used, joining it as shown on the map. Unfortunately, this path is being disturbed at present (1969) by extensions to the quarry but a temporary diversion is indicated by signposts.

trespass route to Beecroft Hall

Leave the path in Sulber Nick when the crosswall comes into sight and walk to the right (no path). In 200 yards the top of a steep limestone scar will be reached: this can most easily be descended at a breach in the rocks 100 yards distant from the wall, which can then be joined and followed south.

scar

22

area devastated by quarry extensions (temporary footpath diversion)

new fence

cairns

23

barn

hall

gate

gate

Beecroft Hall (farm)

gate

ROAD

car park

RIBBLEHEAD and HAWES

railway

Ribble

Crown Hotel

café

ROAD B.6479

800

24

ONE MILE

The stile on the Crummack path is not obvious; it occurs exactly at the point where a stone shooting butt adjoins the wall.

stile

stile

stile

quarry and works

Golden Lion Hotel

Horton in Ribblesdale

SETTLE

CRUMMACK

shooting butt

1200

After crossing the devastated area watch for a stile in the curve of the wall giving access to Beecroft Hall.

There is a recognised pedestrian crossing over the railway lines south of the station buildings. Look left, then right, then left (or vice versa) and if all is quiet summon the last vestiges of energy to make a quick dash across. Don't do it if there's a train coming — it would be such a pity to get bumped off with success almost within sight.

READER'S PERSONAL LOG

This and the next three pages are designed
for the use of readers who may wish to keep
a personal record of their performance of
the walks listed in the book.

Walk	Date	Time start	Time finish	Companions	Weather
1					
2					
3					
4					
5					
6					
7					

Walk	Date	Time		Companions	Weather
		start	finish		
8					
9					
10					
11					
12					
13					
14					
15					
16					
17					

Walk	Date	Time		Companions	Weather
		start	finish		
18					
19					
20					
21					
22					
23					
24					
25					
26					
27					

Walk	Date	Time		Companions	Weather
		start	finish		
28					
29					
30					
31					
32					
33					
34					
HORTON to RIBBLEHEAD					
RIBBLEHEAD to HILL INN					
HILL INN to HORTON					

4
in
three
ges

| Weather | Companion | Time | Day | Date |
		Start/Fin		
				28
				29
				30
				31
				32
				33
				34

Photographs by the author

Moughton

Runscar

clints

erratic, Norber

non-erratic, Thorns Gill

boulders

Diccan Cave

cave of engulfment

Great Douk Cave

cave of debouchure

Attermire Scar

Giggleswick Scar

dry caves

Gaping Gill

Alum Pot

potholes

Trow Gill

dry valley

Moughton

dry waterfall

Thorns Gill

Leck Beck

pools

Easegill

Gordale

ravines

Attermire

Moughton

scars

Beezley Falls

Pecca Falls

waterfalls

Giggleswick

Attermire

summer on the fells

Whernside

Whernside

winter on the fells

Brow Gill

lime kiln

Pikedaw

mine level

Crina Bottom

Bullpot

farmsteads

Middle Washfold

Easegill

waterworn rocks

SYMBOLS AND ABBREVIATIONS USED IN THE MAPS

Good footpath (sufficiently distinct to be followed in mist)

Intermittent footpath (difficult to follow in mist)

No path; route recommended

Walking routes given in this book are not necessarily rights of way

Route on motor road   unenclosed   between walls   between fences

Unenclosed road (off route)

Wall ∘∘∘∘∘∘∘∘∘   Broken wall ∘ ∘ ∘ ∘ ∘   Fence ++++++++   Broken fence ''''''''''''

Limestone clints   Crags   Scree   Boulders

Marshy ground   Trees

Cave or pothole •   Buildings   Contours (at 100' intervals) ......1400...... ......1300......

Summit-cairn ▲   Other (prominent) cairns △   Miles (from starting point) and direction of route ⑤

Stream or river (arrow indicates direction of flow)

Waterfall   Bridge   Railway   Map scale : 2" = 1 mile
North is top of the page

Abbreviations :   O.S. Ordnance Survey   Y.H.A Youth Hostels Association